The Arab Boycott
of Israel

Dan S. Chill

The Praeger Special Studies program—utilizing the most modern and efficient book production techniques and a selective worldwide distribution network—makes available to the academic, government, and business communities significant, timely research in U.S. and international economic, social, and political development.

The Arab Boycott
of Israel

Economic Aggression
and World Reaction

PRAEGER SPECIAL STUDIES IN INTERNATIONAL ECONOMICS AND DEVELOPMENT

Praeger Publishers   New York   Washington   London

Library of Congress Cataloging in Publication Data

Chill, Dan S
    The Arab boycott of Israel.

    (Praeger special studies in international economics
and development)
    Bibliography: p.
    Includes index.
    1. Israel—Foreign economic relations—Arab countries.
2. Arab countries—Foreign economic relations—Israel.
3. Jewish-Arab relations—1917-   I. Title.
HF3861. P24A63   338. 91'17'492705694   76-14431
ISBN 0-275-56810-5

PRAEGER PUBLISHERS
111 Fourth Avenue, New York, N.Y. 10003, U.S.A.

Published in the United States of America in 1976
by Praeger Publishers, Inc.

Printed in the United States of America

To My Wife,
Abigail Susan Chill—
An Exceptional Woman of Valor and Values

"Many daughters have done valiantly,
But thou excellest them all."
(Proverbs 31:29)

Since 1964, when I first became engrossed in the workings of the Arab Boycott of Israel, the world's ignorance of and failure to respond to the looming omnipresence of the Boycott's economic threat have been a cause for deep concern. When, subsequent to the 1973 October war, Arab petrodollars became a predominant economic force in monetary affairs, the world was forced to look anew at the Arab Boycott of Israel and was shocked to discover the Boycott's pervasive structure and extensive objectives. Having no plans of action (or reaction) in reserve upon which to draw, each individual country was forced to react to the Boycott on an ad hoc basis. Due to adverse economic realities facing several countries and their shortsighted governments, the reaction often took the form of unconditional submission to the Boycott's demands.

I write this book not merely (as Winston Churchill put it in *The Gathering Storm*) "to lay the lessons of the past before the future" but to suggest and, ultimately, prove that the power to determine the effectiveness of the Arab Boycott of Israel rests with the political, business, and organizational leadership of countries throughout the world. A concerted offensive by the international community, as a whole, against the Arab Boycott will put an end to the Boycott. The time to act, however, is now.

In the preparation of a book of this nature, intellectual guidance and technical assistance are essential. My sincerest gratitude is extended to Dr. Louis B. Sohn of the Harvard Law School, Dr. Daniel Shimshoni of the Tel Aviv University, Professor Alan Gerson of New England School of Law, Dr. David B. Weisberg of Hebrew Union College, Rev. Dr. Louis C. Gerstein of Congregation Shearith Israel in New York, and David Kamerman, Esq. of New York, all of whose suggestions and comments refined the original manuscript and prepared it for publication. In addition, my appreciation is extended to Dr. James H. Bahti who, in 1969, allowed me to review his monograph on the Boycott and to Ms. Geraldine Shea who typed the final manuscript. Finally and most importantly I cite the efforts, support, and assistance of my wife, Abigail Susan Chill, without whose love, strength, comfort, constructive criticism, and direction this book would not have been written.

CONTENTS

In July 1971, Tuvia Arazi, director of the Political-Economic Planning Division of Israel, emerged from his office in Jerusalem and announced the termination of his division's eleven years of anti-Arab Boycott activity: "The Boycott does us infinitesimal harm now. It is so inefficient and ineffective that we simply don't need this Division any more."[1]

Compared to the Arab League's Boycott Office, headquartered in Damascus, with eighteen branches and a staff of 200, Israel's anti-Boycott office then operated on an annual budget of $15,000 and, even at the height of its activity, was comprised of a staff of seven men and women. At the time of its closure, only two individuals worked in the division, which received its principal aid and support from Jewish organizations throughout the world.[2]

In hindsight, Israel's 1971 decision to close the division and disregard the Arab Boycott was premature. Although the Boycott then appeared as a moribund entity, it has subsequently emerged as a powerful economic organization with which Israel, and the world, must reckon.

One may regard the Arab Boycott as a form of a spider's web. There is resiliency to the Boycott's structure and there are major gaps in the application of its rules and regulations. The web of a spider proves ineffective against insects small enough to permeate its threadlike matrix: it will be destroyed by birds and animals of substantial size and weight. Yet, creatures of medium stature may become entangled and consumed in the web.

So, too, the Arab Boycott has been least successful in its efforts to subjugate individuals and large, multinational corporations. Individuals evoke public sympathy which, in turn, forces the Boycott to withdraw its pressures. Jumbo corporations, through sheer economic power and independence, easily push aside the Boycott's overtures. Small or medium-sized corporations, however, are most often unable to resist the venal temptations of the Boycott.

The Arab League was established on March 22, 1945, by seven Arab countries—Egypt, Iraq, Jordan, Lebanon, Saudi Arabia, Syria, and Yemen.* Today, the Arab League is comprised of twenty nations which, in varying

---

*The Arab League should not be confused with the Organization of Petroleum Exporting Countries (OPEC), which includes many non-Arab nations, and whose unity and strength are derived from a single material resource—oil.

degrees, look upon the league as the catalyst to implement their dreams for Arab political, economic, social, and cultural unity. However, due to the perpetual · political and military squabbles among the Arab states, the sole area in which the league has achieved even a modicum of success has been its economic Boycott.

The Arab Boycott of Israel has had an inestimably adverse effect upon Israel's economy. When performed secretly and against small and medium-sized corporations, or nations greatly dependent on Arab oil, the Boycott has had a certain degree of success. Yet, it is important to note that, even in these instances, the Boycott has shown itself capable of being neutralized when exposed to public scrutiny.

The purpose of this work is to (1) illuminate the darkness and uncertainty enshrouding the Arab Boycott organization; (2) describe its operation in theory and in practice; (3) compare its successes and strengths to its failures and weaknesses; (4) portray local, national, and international reaction to the Boycott; (5) offer an analysis of legal remedies available to individuals, companies, and governments affected by the Boycott's activities; (6) suggest organizational and community responses and countermeasures to the pressures exerted by the Boycott; and (7) assess the Boycott's prospects for future economic influence and importance.

NOTES

1. *Time*, July 19, 1971, p. 17.
2. Ibid.

HISTORY, ORGANIZATION,
AND REGULATIONS

The Arab Boycott of Israel officially began in December 1945, when the Council of the Arab League issued the first formal Boycott declaration. Resolution 16 stated that "Jewish products and manufactured goods shall be considered undesirable to the Arab countries" and called upon all Arab "institutions, organizations, merchants, commission agents and individuals . . . to refuse to deal in, distribute, or consume Zionist products or manufactured goods."[1] Thus, from its official inception, the Boycott deliberately blurred the distinction between products which were Jewish, and those which were Zionist, in origin.

The Arab policy of boycotting Jewish and Zionist goods was not a phenomenon which emerged only after World War II.[2] In 1922, the Fifth Arab Congress, meeting in Nablus, called on Arabs to boycott Jewish business concerns.[3] In October 1929, the First Palestine Arab Women's Congress urged "every Arab to buy nothing from the Jews but land, and to sell them everything but land."[4]

Throughout the 1930s, anti-Zionist boycott declarations increased. In 1931, the World Islamic Congress passed a resolution calling for "the protection of the Holy Places in Palestine by boycotting Zionist goods."[5] The following year, the Arabs attempted to boycott the Jewish-sponsored Tel Aviv Levant Fair and, in March 1933, a general conference, under the auspices of the Arab Executive Committee, proposed a boycott of "Zionist goods, products and commercial premises."[6]

These events led to the Pan-Arab Conference held at Bludan, Syria, in September 1937. A resolution was passed calling the boycott of Jews "a patriotic duty."[7] It was apparently effective. In 1937, there were reports of very few Arab customers entering Jewish shops in the Middle East.[8]

1

Nonetheless, during the prewar period, exhortations and resolutions, rather than actual deeds, predominated and, with the suspension of boycott activities during the war, the situation remained quiescent until 1945.

The December 1945 pronouncement noted above embodied the policy developed by Awni Abdul Hadi, then one of the most influential members of the Arab Higher Committee.[9] The following February, the Arab League Council established a permanent Boycott Committee "to implement and enforce" the earlier Boycott decision and to study plans and proposals which might be submitted in the near future.[10]

The Boycott Committee's suggestions appeared on June 12, 1946, in the following resolution of the council:

> The [Permanent Boycott] Committee suggests to the Council that it should recommend to the [Arab] Governments the adoption of the following measures:
>   *First.* The establishment of boycott offices in each state of the League for local supervision; these offices should be in constant touch with the Permanent Boycott Committee in Cairo and with other boycott committees. . . .
>   *Third.* The allocation of 50 percent of the value of confiscated goods to guides and officials in order to encourage . . . secret information about the smuggling of Zionist goods.[11]

In order to temper its negative aspects, the resolution added:

> . . . [T]he boycott should . . . also be positive. . . . [T]he Arabs . . . should establish industries having sound economic bases to replace Zionist industries so that Arabs of Palestine may rely on Arab production without suffering any harm on account of the boycott of Zionist goods. . . .[12]

Two aspects of this document are of special interest. The first is the use of the words "suggests" and "recommend" in the opening sentence of the council's resolution. Since 1950 the Arab countries have only been requested, not required, to implement the Boycott.[13]

Moreover, the council had been informed that an international trade conference, meeting concurrently in the United States, would submit a proposal asking countries to refrain "from fostering or organizing boycotts of member states." Yet, the Arab League's Internal Committee urged the Arab states "immediately to adopt a unified policy so that the means of implementing the boycott of Zionism will be retained irrespective of the principle" advocated at the trade conference.[14]

In 1949, the Arab League Council voted to move its headquarters from Cairo to Damascus.[15] The major task of the Damascus Central Boycott Office was the maintenance of "security of communications between the [affiliated] [B]oycott Offices in each country" and the coordination of activities in the local offices.[16] Each participating Arab government, including any nonmember of the Arab League, was requested to appoint a liaison officer to the Central Boycott Office in Damascus. In addition, and in some ways similar to the condition extant under the Cairo Central Office,

> ... each participating state was to organize a national boycott office, under the supervision of the Damascus headquarters. The Boycott commissioner was empowered to convene annual meetings of the liaison officers. He was also directed to make quarterly reports to the Secretary-General [of the Arab League] on the progress of the boycott, copies of which were to be provided for member states.[17]

In actuality, two meetings of the Boycott liaison officers were held each year. These semiannual meetings helped coordinate Boycott policies and programs throughout the world, under the general guidance of the Arab League Council and the League's Economic Council.[18]

Before the shift to Damascus was completed,[19] the General Boycott Committee, in conjunction with its branch offices,[20] announced a change in basic policy.[21] Before the Egyptian decree of February 6, 1950,[22] the Boycott's purpose was to bar Arab importation of Israeli goods.[23] Following the decree, which contained a long list of goods that were forbidden passage through the Suez Canal,[24] the committee expanded its drive "to include shipping services in an attempt [not only] to obstruct the flow of refugees from Arab countries to Israel,"[25] but to hinder the flow of trade in and out of Israel. Thus, the primary boycott of Israel became a secondary boycott of those companies dealing with Israel.

In September 1950, the decree was extended to require a guarantee by ship and oil tanker captains that their vessels would not ultimately discharge any of their cargo in an Israeli port. Also, submission of log books by tankers proceeding southward through the canal became obligatory. Vessels found to have called on Israeli ports were placed on a blacklist (note the appearance of a blacklist for the first time) and denied supplies, fuel, and repair facilities in Egyptian ports.[26] If these regulations were resisted in any way, the ship would be deemed to have lost its neutrality by reason of the "hostile act" and, even if no contraband were found on board, the ship would be seized and its cargo impounded. Eventually, on November 28, 1953, the definition of the word "contraband" was broadened to include "foodstuffs and all other commodities which are likely to strengthen the war potential of the Zionists in Palestine in any way whatsoever."[27]

It is of interest to note that, officially, the Boycott has never applied to foreign firms that sell noncapital goods on an export basis:

Any firm that chose to sell through its own sales department, through export merchants, combination export managers, or some other manner was allowed to do so without endangering its capacity for doing business in Arab nations. The Arab League believed that investment in Israel would lead to the country's growth, while imports from a third country would aggravate the persistent balance of payments problems that Israel has faced since its founding.[28]

Yet, at least one authority on the Arab Boycott, James H. Bahti, states that he is "aware of cases where firms engaged in 'normal trade' have received questionnaires from the Central Boycott Office and other Boycott officials."[29] Moreover, it is unclear why, in 1953, the Boycott was extended to ships delivering food and other commodities to Israel if, as the Arabs allege, imports to Israel aggravate its balance of payments problems.

Even as late as 1961, statements by regional Boycott officials referred to "firms doing business with Israel." In fact, an April 1966 Arab publication stated unequivocally that the Boycott provisions "apply to any acts of trade or commerce with Israel."[30]

In sum, the Arabs, themselves, have been unable, or unwilling, to apply the Boycott regulations with precision and uniformity. However, it is clear from the publicized 1970 blacklist that firms doing business with Israel, notwithstanding balance of payment considerations, have been boycotted by the Arabs.

In September 1952, the Arab League Council recommended the Boycott of companies that have branches in Israel[31] and the surveillance of all sea, land, and air communication and trade contrary to the Boycott's rules. The council also indicated that, henceforth, the Boycott Office was to be included in the newly created Palestine Department within the office of the League's secretary general.[32]

The 1952 council interdiction was adopted soon thereafter and incorporated in the 1959 announcement of the General Union of the Arab Chambers of Commerce, Industry and Agriculture, which declared that the following types of firms would be placed on the Arab Boycott's blacklist: (1) firms which have branch factories in Israel; (2) firms which have assembly plants in Israel, including firms whose agents assemble their products in Israel, even by their own special arrangements; (3) firms which have in Israel either general agencies or main offices for their Middle Eastern operations; (4) firms which give their patents, trademarks, or copyrights to Israeli companies; (5) firms, and public and private organizations, which buy shares of Israeli companies or factories; (6) consultants and technical firms who offer their services to Israel.[33] "If a firm has breached any of the above regulations but without having known of their existence, it is offered the choice of closing down the prohibited operation . . . or being blacklisted by the Arab governments."[34]

Since 1959, new causes for blacklisting have been added: direct or indirect help to Israel's economic growth or war potential; failure to promptly answer inquiries from Arab Boycott authorities; manufacture anywhere in the world of goods of Israeli-made materials or components; sale of goods, anywhere, that are identical to goods imported from Israel (the reason for this is to prevent re-export); investment in an already blacklisted company (an example of tertiary boycott); sale of products that contain a motor or generator made by a black-listed firm, or components manufactured by a blacklisted firm, worth 35 percent or more of the value, or constituting more than 50 percent of the components of such unit;[35] sale of stock to citizens of Israel; appointing an Israeli as a corporate officer; joining a foreign-Israeli chamber of commerce in Israel or abroad; lending money or providing financial aid in any form to Israeli entities; and taking part in or supporting propaganda activities on behalf of Israel. The latter three "offenses" apply to firms and their officers.[36] In addition, several companies received warnings in 1964 that they would be blacklisted if they exhibited at the Tel Aviv trade fair.[37] (For a complete list of American firms on the Saudi Arabian blacklist of 1970, see Appendix F.)

A final group of Boycott regulations are of interest due to the apparatus through which they are implemented. Using Iraq as an example, imports and exports to and from that country

> . . . require special licenses, certificates of origin and destination, and endorsement by Iraqi or other Arab diplomatic personnel in the for-eign countries involved. Iraq also sends to the general boycott office in Damascus lists of her exports to foreign countries, including America, so that Arab missions in these countries may check to see that none of the Iraqi goods are trans-shipped in violation of boycott regulations.[38]

Examples of the affidavit and the negative certificate of origin, as well as the questionnaire sent out by Boycott offices to firms suspected of dealing with Israel will be found in Appendix A. For the "mechanics" of the boycott see Appendix B.

THE BOYCOTT'S OBJECTIVES

The Arabs contend that the Boycott[39] is a "defensive measure,"[40] made necessary by the fact that, in the past, Israel forcibly expelled 1.4 million Arabs and took their properties; that, at present, Israel controls thousands of square miles of Arab territory, and Israel's ground and air forces constantly raid Arab frontier villages; and that, in the future, Israel plans to expand further, both politically and economically.[41] If we grant these allegations, we see that the Arabs "are . . . doing no more than trying to deny Israel that economic power which might enable it to realize a new step in its attempt for the achievement of its distorted dream of domination."[42]

In addition, many Arab leaders observe the existing situation in the following way: "A military solution to the problem does not seem easy. But there is a
weapon that does not involve steel and fire, a weapon that will help us win—the
Arab Boycott of Israel."[43] In sum, the Arab League's objectives are

> to maintain in the Arab area a tight boycott and blockade of Israel,
> and to bring all influence to bear on other Afro-Asian [as well as
> Western] states to cooperate in keeping Israel from extending its
> trade or influence, from obtaining membership in international bod-
> ies, and from gaining recognition as a nation. . . . Arabs . . . Take the
> position that if they continue to isolate Israel from its neighbors and
> prevent it from putting down roots in the Middle East, meanwhile
> developing their own strength and influence, time will work to their
> advantage. . . .[44]

While the Arab Boycott's main effort is "expended on Israel's economic
strangulation,"[45] and the Middle East Trade Council's "declared function is to
encourage trade with each of the Middle East countries—except Israel,"[46] the
Arab countries continually stress the Boycott's "clear distinction between a boycott based on religious discrimination and that based upon specific kinds of
material aid to the State of Israel."[47] This alleged distinction is expressed in the
following manner:

> [The Boycott] is not inspired by racial motives. . . . [It is] directed
> against *Israel*, but *not* against the Jews. Indeed there are many Jew-
> ish citizens in most of the Arab states who are unmolested and
> prosperous. . . .
>   Jewish firms outside Israel receive from the Arabs the same treat-
> ment as non-Jewish firms. There is no discrimination. *Any* firm,
> irrespective of the creed or race of its owners, shareholders, or man-
> agers will be able to deal with Arab countries, so long as it does not
> breach the regulations of the Arab Boycott of Israel.[48]

The opposite position, presented by the World Jewish Congress, maintains
that "Arab governments boycott firms with even a single Jewish employee. . . ."[49]
In addition, the Public Affairs Institute in Washington, D.C. has stated that "the
boycott was applied to foreign firms having Jewish directors."[50]

In February 1975, in response to Boycott pressure, the Overseas Private
Investment Corporation (OPIC), a governmental agency which promotes U.S.
trade projects in developing countries, requested an American business firm to
withdraw the name of its Jewish vice president from a list of proposed partici-
pants in an OPIC mission to the Middle East and North Africa.[51] In May 1975,
negotiations for a technical assistance contract between the Massachusetts Institute of Technology and Saudi Arabia were terminated. This resulted from Saudi

Arabia's refusal to sign a contract which contained a clause prohibiting Saudi Arabia from denying a visa to any member of the project's working staff or academic personnel because of his or her religious affiliation.[52]

In December 1975, the American Jewish Congress revealed a directive from the Saudi Arabian Ministry of Foreign Affairs to the Aramco oil consortium. The directive stated that Saudi Arabia would issue visas to Aramco employees but not to "undesirable persons, it being understood that the undesirable persons include the Jews."[53]

NOTES

1. Frank Gervasi, *The Case for Israel* (New York: Viking Press, 1967), p. 130. See also Robert W. MacDonald, *The League of Arab States: A Study in the Dynamics of Regional Organization* (Princeton, N.J.: Princeton University Press, 1965), pp. 118-19.

2. James H. Bahti, *The Arab Economic Boycott of Israel* (Washington, D.C.: The Brookings Institution, 1967), p. 1.

3. Ibid. According to a detailed study of the Palestine problem made by the Esco Foundation, in May 1921, "a boycott, commenced by the Arabs, soon became mutual." Esco Foundation, *Palestine—A Study of Jewish, Arab and British Policies*, vol. 1 (New Haven, Conn.: Yale University Press, 1947), p. 270.

4. M. E. T. Mogannam, *The Arab Woman* (London: Hubert Joseph, 1937), p. 72.

5. Esco Foundation, op. cit., vol. 2, p. 761, quoted in Bahti, op. cit., p. 1. See also Arnold J. Toynbee, *Survey of International Affairs, 1934* (London: Oxford University Press, 1934), p. 107.

6. *Palestine Royal Commission Report,* Commission Mandate Documents (CMD) 5479 (London: His Majesty's Stationery Office, 1937), p. 83.

7. R. G. Woolbert, "Pan-Arabism and the Palestine Problem," *Foreign Affairs* (January 1938): 317.

8. *Palestine Royal Commission Report,* op. cit., p. 146.

9. Gervasi, op. cit., p. 130.

10. Bahti, op. cit., p. 3.

11. M. Khalil, *The Arab States and the Arab League*, vol. II (Beirut: Kahayats, 1955), pp. 162-63. See also Fred J. Khouri, *The Arab—Israeli Dilemma* (Syracuse, N.Y.: Syracuse University Press, 1968), p. 35.

12. Khalil, op. cit., and Arab League Council, Resolution 70, sess. 4, sched. 6, June 12, 1946, pp. 18-19.

13. This is true of all Arab League resolutions as well. For a text of the Arab League pact, see *American Journal of International Law* 39, supp. (1945):266ff, or UNCIO (United Nations Committee on International Organizations) document 72, III/4/1. See also Paul Seabury, "The League of Arab States: Debacle of a Regional Arrangement," *International Organization* (February 1949):633-42.

14. Khalil, op. cit., p. 163.

15. *New Outlook* (Middle East monthly) 4, no. 5, (March-April 1961): 33.

16. Arab League Council, Resolution 357, May 19, 1951, as cited in Egyptian Society of International Law, *Egypt and the United Nations* (New York: Manhattan Publishing Co., 1957).

17. MacDonald, op. cit., pp. 133-34.

18. Ibid., p. 123.

19. Robert E. Weigand, "The Arab League Boycott of Israel," *Michigan State University Business Topics* (Spring 1968): 75.

20. Business International, May 31, 1957. The local Boycott Office's activities usually fall within the responsibilities of each country's Ministry of Commerce. Note, however, that Iraq's Boycott Office is in the Ministry of Foreign Affairs; Lebanon's Boycott activities, although under the Ministry of National Economy, are subject to the final approval of the Council of Ministers; and the Boycott apparatus of the United Arab Republic "operates within the Ministry of War." See, generally, Bahti's excellent description of regional Boycott offices, in op. cit., pp. 20-23.

21. It is of interest to note that MacDonald, op. cit., pp. 118-19, feels that "the boycott was originally envisaged as a simple operation to prevent smuggling and the Arab League Boycott Office was headed by an Egyptian Coast Guard officer until 1951. But since 1948, when Israel established itself as a state, the boycott has been elaborated into an instrument of economic warfare by which all financial and commercial transactions between Arab states and Israel are banned. . . ."

22. *Egyptian Official Journal,* no. 36 (April 8, 1950). It should be noted that, also in 1950, the Arab Joint Defense and Economic Cooperation Treaty was signed and became operative in 1952. This was an attempt by Egypt to revitalize the league by introducing a collective security pact.

23. *Near East Report,* "The Arab Boycott Involves Americans" (suppl.), May 1965, p. B-2.

24. Abba Eban, *The Voice of Israel* (New York: Horizon Press, 1957), p. 256.

25. Gervasi, op. cit., p. 131; see also *Facts* (Anti-Defamation League) 14, no. 2 (February 1961): 181.

26. Eban, op. cit., p. 257.

27. Ibid., p. 258.

28. Weigand, op. cit.

29. Bahti, op. cit., p. 10. Bahti adds in a footnote on p. 71 that "it may be, as one Arab publication has stated, that such inquiries are intended to obtain 'clarification with regard to the nature and extent of these dealings' and that the subject will be closed if the dealings are of a 'purely commercial nature.'" *The Arab World* 11, no. 2 (February 1964): 2.

30. *For the Record,* (Arab Information Center, New York), April 25, 1966, p. 2, cited in Bahti, op. cit., p. 10.

31. Arab League Council Resolution 482, September 1952. According to one authority, those firms with branches both in Israel and in the Arab states were exempt; yet, this distinction was abolished in 1953. B.Y. Boutros-Ghali, "The Arab League: Ten Years of Struggle," *International Concilliation* (May 1954): 418, cited in Bahti, op. cit., p. 70. n. 12.

32. Bahti, op. cit., p. 5.

33. General Union of the Arab Chambers of Commerce, Industry and Agriculture, *Arab Boycott of Israel: Its Grounds and Its Regulations* (Beirut, 1959), pp. 2-3.

34. Ibid., p. 3.

35. "General Principles for Boycott of Israel," sec. 15, June 1972, Arab League, General Secretariat, Head Office for the Boycott of Israel, Damascus (hereafter cited as "General Principles for Boycott of Israel").

36. Business International,"Coping with the Arab Boycott of Israel," Management Monographs (New York: Business International, 1964), pp. 3-5; see also *Facts,* op. cit.

37. Ibid., p. 5.

38. Business International, May 31, 1957. The Government of Bahrain, too, requires that invoices from shippers be accompanied by certificates obtained from chambers of commerce or Arab embassies declaring that the goods are not from a Jewish source. *Facts* 12, no. 2 (March-April 1957): 102.

39. For a precise review of the Arab Boycott's general principles and regulations, see Rashad Mourad, "The Arab Boycott—Its Application," *American-Arab Trade Newsletter* (New York), Spring-Summer 1966, pp. 5-6.

40. General Union of the Arab Chambers of Commerce, Industry and Agriculture, op. cit., pp. 1-2.

41. New York *Times,* October 16, 1957; see also New York *Times,* February 18, 1960.

42. General Union of the Arab Chambers of Commerce, Industry and Agriculture, op. cit., pp. 1-2. See also Oded Remba, "The Arab Boycott: A Study in Total Economic Warfare," *Midstream* 6, no. 3 (Summer 1960): 48-49.

43. Hutik Muhamed Ali Aluba, *Palestine and Human Conscience* (Cairo: Dar Elhalal, 1964), p. 187, as cited in Yehoshafat Harkabi, *Emdat Ha-aravim Bisihsuh Yisroel-Arav* [The Arabs' Position in the Arab-Israeli Conflict] (Tel Aviv: Dvir Co., 1968), p. 39. The English translation here of Aluba's remarks is my own translation of Harkabi's Hebrew version of the original Arab text. The reader must, therefore, excuse the imprecision which may exist in the translation.

44. Charles D. Cremeans, *The Arabs and the World* (New York: Frederick A. Praeger, 1963), p. 195.

45. J. K. Banerji, *The Middle East in World Politics* (Calcutta: The World Press Private, 1960), p. 203. See also *Le Commerce du Levant* (Beirut), August 1954.

46. Abba Eban, "The Answer to Arab Boycott," in *The Israel Yearbook, 1966* (Jerusalem: Israel Yearbook Publications, 1966), p. 20.

47. Clarence L. Coleman, Jr., "Boycott Not Religious, Arabs Tell State Department," *Issues* (Spring 1962): 79-80.

48. General Union of the Arab Chambers of Commerce, Industry and Agriculture, op. cit., p. 2.

49. World Jewish Congress, *Evidence of the Arab War in Peacetime Against Israel* (Tel Aviv: Hadfus Haklali, 1957).

50. Public Affairs Institute, "Regional Development for Regional Peace," mimeographed (Washington, D.C.: Public Affairs Institute, 1957), p. 276.

51. Arnold Forster, "The Arab Boycott: An Interim Report," *ADL Bulletin* (June 1975): 2. It is of interest to note that OPIC has issued $54 million of insurance coverage in Israel. Jerusalem *Post,* June 27, 1975.

52. *Jewish Advocate,* May 15, 1975; Los Angeles *Times,* December 1, 1975.

53. Jerusalem *Post,* December 18, 1975.

PURVIEW

The following discussion will attempt to depict the effect of the Arab Boycott's political and economic strategy upon individuals, corporations, and foreign governments. However, the word "strategy" connotes an overall plan, a grand design for the ultimate successful achievement of one's goal. This schema is not to be found as one views the Arab Boycott in action.

The table on the following page presents a model of the Arab Boycott activities. The reader will immediately be struck by the contrasting results of the Arab measures. The Boycott has had its greatest success in forcing foreign oil corporations to comply with its dictates due to the Middle East's control over two-thirds of the world's known oil reserves. With the exception of Iran, all Middle Eastern countries are unified in their resolve to close the supply of oil to Israel. More important, there have been no political repercussions resulting from the oil embargo directed toward Israel. Since most foreign governments have taken for granted that the Arabs will not allow their own soil's resources to aid Israel, adverse world opinion has been minimal. Thus, Israel has been forced to import oil by tankers rather than through the less expensive pipelines of Iraq, Saudi Arabia, and Jordan.

A similar success is found when Boycott officials resort to diplomatic confrontation and pressure. As long as meetings are held privately, Boycott attempts remain unpublicized. Even those countries that are unsympathetic can usually be counted upon not to bring the Arab overtures into the public domain.

So, too, in their dealings with the shipping industries of foreign countries the Arabs, generally, are able to achieve significant economic results without adverse publicity. This is due to the fact that most of the shipping industry needs Arab port facilities, and looks forward to the use, once again, of the Suez Canal.

EFFECTIVENESS OF ARAB BOYCOTT ACTIVITIES

Party Involved	Economic Success	Political Success	Ultimate Resolution of the Confrontation
Shipping	Inability of Israel to have its trade pass through the canal causes it economic hardship	Adverse world opinion, yet no major reaction due to world's need for the canal	Backfire–canal, between 1967 and 1975, was closed to all ships and Egypt received $280 million per year from Libya, Kuwait, and Saudi Arabia to offset its losses due to canal's closure
Airlines	Mixed–airlines needing Arab airports have capitulated; most have not	Depends on sympathy of nation in which airline is based. On whole, has caused very little discussion	Japan Air Lines capitulation; possible TWA monetary payment; yet, on whole, total disregard by firms
Individuals	None	Invariably adverse world reaction due to great deal of publicity regarding Arab pressures	Failure
Oil corporations	Able to force Middle East countries and foreign oil companies to comply with Boycott	Except for Iran, relatively successful	Israeli economic loss
Foreign governments (contracts and agreements)	Depends on an individual country's assessment of its economic (and political) needs for Arab market	Until 1960, good success rate; in 1960s and 1970s, more adverse reaction except in Japan and later in Great Britain	Unfavorable individual country reactions but no concerted international efforts to stop Arab attempts
Diplomatic pressures on governments	Succeeds with those countries that are sympathetic or economically dependent upon Arabs	Attains certain measure of support without having action placed in public eye	Successful whether or not agreement is reached because discussions are kept secret
Giant corporations (excluding oil, Japanese, and a number of British companies)	None	Unfavorable repercussions	Failure

Source: Compiled by the author.

There are, however, many Arab Boycott activities that have not only failed economically but have been politically disastrous. Boycott attempts to blacklist individuals (actors, celebrities, officers of financial institutions, and so on) invariably have led to massive newspaper coverage and public scandal. Although several airlines need Middle East airports for refueling and repair, most refuse to accede to Boycott demands. Similarly, efforts to influence other large, international corporations have failed due to the economic ability of these firms to outlast the Arab countries and to coordinate their reactions to Boycott demands with those of the public. Finally, the Arab attempt to force compliance upon foreign governments through contracts and trade agreements, although successful through the 1950s, has met increasing resistance as the public increases its knowledge and awareness of the Boycott's activities. Thus, the Arabs, by overextending the scope of the Boycott, thereby increasing its notoriety, have decreased the Boycott's effectiveness.

The remainder of this chapter will portray, in greater detail, the broad areas encompassed within the Boycott's ambit, and its political, economic, and psychological successes and failures.

GENERAL ACTIVITY

The Arab Boycott Committee's activities are extensive in scope and design. The Boycott machinery is used to cajole, harass, and threaten individuals, airlines, shipping lines, small, large, and giant corporations, governmental agencies, and states.

One of the most effective Boycott activities was the Egyptian blockade practice with regard to Israeli cargoes traversing the Suez Canal.* The Constantinople Convention of 1888, signed by Great Britain, Germany, Austria-Hungary, Spain, France, Italy, the Netherlands, Russia, and Turkey, proclaimed that "the Suez Maritime Canal shall always be free and open in time of war as in time of peace, to every vessel of commerce or of war, without distinction of flag. . . . The canal shall never be subjected to the exercise of the right of blockade."[1] Yet in direct contradiction of the 1888 convention, Egypt, through 1975, maintained in the UN Security Council that, as an active belligerent against Israel, it was entitled to exercise the right of visit, search, and seizure for legitimate self-defense.[2] This contention was rejected by the Security Council as early as September 1, 1951, when it called upon Egypt "to terminate the

---

*Since the six-day war in 1967, the world had been forced to share with Israel the inconvenience created by the physical closure of the canal. The canal was reopened by Egypt in 1975.

restrictions on the passage of international commercial shipping and goods through the Suez Canal wherever bound and to cease all interference with such shipping."[3] Almost three years later, Russia vetoed another Security Council resolution condemning the Egyptian blockade against Israeli shipping.[4]

Despite these international legal efforts, Egypt continued its blockade practices, including the confiscation of a cargo of Israel-bound meat on the Norwegian vessel *Rimfrost*; the seizure of building materials and Israeli-manufactured automobiles from the Greek vessel *Parnon*; the confiscation and seizure of a cargo of meat and hides from the Italian vessel *Franca Maria* and of clothing and bicycles from the Norwegian ship *Laritan*; and the detention and seizure of the Israeli vessel *Bat Galim,* which was carrying meat, plywood, and hides from Massawa to Haifa.[5] In the case of the *Bat Galim,* the crew was put in jail on a charge of opening fire on Egyptian fishermen at the entrance to the canal. The Egyptian-Israeli Mixed Armistice Commission rejected Egypt's charge and the Security Council was influential in the release of the crew. Yet, the cargo was never returned and Egypt consigned the ship to its navy.[6]

Following the 1975 reopening of the Suez Canal, and as part of the 1975 interim agreement between Israel and Egypt, ships carrying goods to or from Israel have been allowed to transit the canal. Yet, although admitting that the Boycott had no authority to prevent such ships from traversing the canal, Boycott Commissioner General Mohammed Mahmood Mahgoub announced that "these vessels will not be allowed to anchor in any Arab port and will not be serviced."[7] As an example, Mahgoub cited the Greek freighter *Olympos,* which went through the canal on November 2, 1975, carrying a consignment of Rumanian cement to Eilat.

Mahgoub also sought Egypt's assent to bar blacklisted vessels from docking at the ports of Suez and Port Said, at the southern and northern ends of the Suez Canal, when sailing through the waterway. Egypt, however, refused to accede to the Boycott official's call, tacitly agreeing with the legal opinion of Meir Rosenne, legal advisor to Israel's Foreign Ministry, that essential services, such as piloting and refueling, are the sine qua non for passage through the canal and, hence, Egypt's refusal to offer such services would be a violation of the interim agreement.[8]

The boycott of ships extends to Tripoli, Libya, where vessels have been "forbidden to land because they had formerly visited an Israeli port."[9] In August 1957, *Fortune* magazine listed one hundred ships of foreign registry on the blacklist. Today the figure is less certain.

The fact that the Boycott blacklists ships, as well as shipping companies, is of some interest. American Export Lines, Inc. (AEL) is the largest American-flag carrier of freight to and from Israel and has maintained regular service to Israel since 1948. Yet, AEL ships calling at Israeli ports do not call at Arab ports and vice versa.[10]

On March 4, 1975, the Anti-Defamation League of B'nai B'rith (ADL) made public a Boycott activity that has been practiced for almost two decades.

Typewritten forms, attesting that a given vessel carrying goods from the United States to a customer in an Arab country is not on the Arab Boycott's blacklist, must be furnished sellers before letters of credit will be honored by Arab banks. Fourteen U.S. shipping companies were shown to have complied with the Boycott's demand in this regard, three of which companies, American Export Lines, Inc., the Waterman Steamship Corporation, and the Lykes Brothers Steamship Company, have received, and continue to receive, subsidies for some or all of their routes from the Maritime Administration of the U.S. Department of Commerce.[11]

The Boycott regulations regarding air travel, in open defiance of the International Convention Governing Civil Aviation and the International Air Service Transit Agreement,[12] state that planes making use of Israel's facilities are forbidden to fly over Arab territory, seek weather information, or obtain rescue services. In addition, Arab countries, in general, have threatened uncooperative airlines with antiaircraft fire.[13]

Yet, the Arabs' success vis-a-vis commercial airlines has been mixed. In the late 1950s, the local Boycott offices gave Air France a great deal of trouble regarding a plane-lease agreement with El Al.[14] Relations deteriorated and on March 17, 1957, Syria ordered all Air France offices in Syria closed and banned all Air France planes from Syria.[15] For the next two years, Air France attempted to remove its name from the Arab blacklist and, in September 1959, finally succeeded in doing so by breaking off its negotiations with El Al to establish an operational tie-up between the two airlines.[16] At the present time, Air France flies to Israel. However, a series of advertisements, appearing in the French newspapers in December 1974, displayed a map and listing of destinations to which Air France flies in the Middle East, and conspicuous in its omission was Ben Gurion International Airport, Lod, Israel.

Meanwhile, in 1965, the Arabs forbade Tabso, the Bulgarian national airline, from flying over or landing in their countries after the company established a twice-monthly air link connecting Sofia and Tel Aviv, the first air service between an Eastern bloc country and Israel.[17] In 1967, Bulgaria cancelled this air link but, later, an air agreement between Rumania and Israel was consummated. The Boycott's ban on Tarom, the Rumanian national airline, along with its sanctions against the Scandinavian Air System (SAS) and Swissair, have not deterred these airlines from continuing their flights to and from Israel.[18] In addition, one must regard with interest the case of Trans World Airlines (TWA), having offices and offering its services in both Cairo and Tel Aviv.[19] The fact that in this case no hint of blacklisting has been raised may be due to diverse factors, ranging from political or economic expediency to a possible Arab-TWA monetary arrangement.

The blacklisting of individuals has often given adverse publicity to Arab League activities within a certain country. A great stir was caused in France by a Boycott Committee letter sent to General Pierre Koenig, former French minister of defense, demanding his resignation from the chairmanship of the boards of two French oil companies, due to his membership in the Franco-Israel Alliance. The letter remains unanswered to this day.[20] A Boycott questionnaire (see Appendix A) sent to the chairman of the board of directors of Verkoopkantoor Van der Heum, N.V., of The Hague, the Netherlands, on November 13, 1955, elicited a similar nonresponse.[21]

The most famous instance of Arab Boycott pressure upon an individual was the Mancroft affair of December 1963. Lord Mancroft, a 49-year-old British business leader from a prominent Jewish family, resigned from the London board of the Norwich Union Insurance Societies, one of Great Britain's biggest insurance groups, because of Arab pressure. The company, having assets of $750 million, and premiums of $280 million, a very small fraction of which came from the Arab world, told Mancroft that his position would "jeopardize its prospects in the Arab countries."[22] The New York *Times* felt that the Arab pressure was mainly due to Mancroft's other professional activities. He was chairman of Global Tours, Ltd., a travel agency that had acquired a controlling interest in Charles S. Robinson, Ltd., of Manchester. The latter did a substantial business in Israel.[23] In addition, Mancroft was a director in Great Universal Stores, Ltd., one of Great Britain's largest merchandising organizations, controlled by Sir Isaac Wolfson, who had financial and philanthropic interests in Israel. Thus, again we see emerging the tertiary aspects of the Arab Boycott.

While the British government's Foreign Office protested to the Saudi Arabian, Iraqi, and Libyan ambassadors to England, and announced that it "strongly resented" and "strongly disapproved" of the Arab pressures,[24] Mohammed Mahgoub (commissioner general of the Arab League's Boycott Committee) urged member states of the league to insure their goods with the Norwich Union Insurance group.[25]

As may be expected, the public reaction to Norwich Union's behavior was negative. The firm received hundreds of letters cancelling policies and demanding the resignation of the board. Caught in a dilemma, Norwich opted to pacify the majority of its clientele by asking Lord Mancroft to return, despite the league's warning that such action immediately would place Norwich on the blacklist.[26] Mancroft rejected the firm's offer[27] and, soon thereafter, two of Norwich's directors, Sir Hughe Knatchbull-Hugessen, a retired diplomat, and Sir Charles Mott-Radclyffe, a Conservative member of Parliament, resigned because of the willingness of the company to yield to Arab pressure.[28]

Stung by the bad publicity they had received, the Arabs quickly retaliated. Syria and Jordan blacklisted fifty and forty-nine British companies, respectively, and forbade their owners and directors from entering the two countries.[29] Yet, since the British government immediately pledged aid to the firms affected, and because of Norwich's besmirched public image, most British companies, following the Mancroft affair, stiffened their position vis-a-vis the Boycott.[30] Nevertheless, the newly acquired Arab oil wealth, along with the instability currently permeating Great Britain's economy, has had the effect of significantly shifting the stance of many British companies with regard to the Boycott.[31]

Famous individuals, including actors, actresses, entertainers, and motion picture producers, have found their works,[32] or themselves, blacklisted for activities that have aided the State of Israel. On April 7, 1954, *Variety* reported that the film companies Metro-Goldwyn-Mayer, Columbia, Universal, and Paramount had been investigated by various Boycott offices as to their personnel. Syria, Lebanon, and Jordan sent letters seeking to establish "the number of Jews employed by the four," and "whether their 'principals' are Christian or Jewish."[33]

In 1959, Elizabeth Taylor's movies were banned in all Arab countries because she had purchased $100,000 in Israel Bonds.[34] Danny Kaye has been on the blacklist for many years and, in 1961, Eddie Cantor was blacklisted due to his "Zionist affiliations and material support of Israel."[35] Two years later, Joanne Woodward, Steve Allen, and French singer-actress Juliette Greco were banned, along with all movies in which they appeared.[36] In addition, since 1965, all of Sophia Loren's films have been barred by the Boycott Committee because she starred in *Judith,* a film based on the 1948 Arab-Israeli War.[37] Finally, all enterprises associated with Otto Preminger have been blacklisted by the Jordanian Ministerial Council.[38]

In recognition of the fact that the psychological gain resulting from such extensive blacklisting may be offset by the economic effect upon Arab movie theater entrepreneurs, the Arabs have somewhat relaxed the blacklisting of movies and individual movie stars (as described later in this chapter).

The Boycott has been most effective in the oil industry. As we have seen, no oil tanker was allowed through the Suez Canal if its destination was Israel. In 1960, the Arab League symbolically extended its Boycott to include Iran because of the Shah's reaffirmation of his country's de facto recognition of Israel[39] and its willingness to supply Israel with oil. This oil was, and continues to be, delivered to the southern port of Eilat, thereby entirely avoiding the Suez Canal. Five months later the major oil-producing members asked the league to prevent the Western oil companies that sell Iranian oil from shipping to Eilat.[40]

In 1958, Royal Dutch Shell sold the Shell Oil Company of Palestine (now trading as Paz) because of "commercial considerations" and, later in the same year, Shell and the British Petroleum Company sold a jointly owned refinery in Haifa.[41] In addition, since the 1950s, Saudi Arabia, along with other Arab countries, has prevented foreign oil companies from employing Jewish nationals, even in the companies' enterprises outside the Arab world.[42]

The influence of the Boycott apparatus on foreign governmental actions was, at least in the 1950s, impressive as well as sobering. Again Saudi Arabia set the standard by refusing

... to allow American Jews to be stationed on its territory as members of the United States armed forces at Dhahran Air Base. The agreement, signed in 1951 and renewed in 1957, requires the United States Mission to submit a 'detailed list of the names and identities' of its members and employees so that it will not include 'individuals objectionable to the Saudi Arabian Government.'[43]

The U.S. Department of State expressed confidence that these restrictions would fade as Arab-Israeli relations improved. The Anti-Defamation League disagreed and protested the Saudi Arabian government's action as well as the State Department's timid response.[44] As will be shown, organizational pressures have forced the State Department to reassess its position in this regard.

Another means employed by the United States to indirectly abet the Boycott's cause can be seen in connection with the so-called Haifa Clause of January 1960. Until then the military sea transportation policy charter agreements stipulated that the U.S. Navy could cancel the charter of a ship, require the substitution of another ship of similar size, or nominate another loading port, in the event a vessel was prevented from loading by local authorities because of previous trade with Israel.[45] The Haifa Clause now added to the agreements tanker owners, who were refused accomodations as a result of the Arab Boycott, for any penalties resulting from the delays in fulfilling the agreements.[46] Thus, in effect, shipowners were forced to choose whether their ships would serve Israel or the Arab countries.

On February 4, 1960, only two weeks after the Haifa Clause achieved notoriety in the American press, it became known that the U.S. Department of Agriculture and its subsidiary, the Commodity Credit Corporation (CCC), were sanctioning a clause prohibiting U.S. dry-cargo vessels from calling at Israeli ports. Since such shipments to Egypt were under the Agricultural Trade, Development and Assistance Act, the American taxpayer, unknowingly, was supporting this practice, which had freight charges alone of $4.54 million.[47]

On February 18, 1960, the navy withdrew the Haifa Clause from its oil-cargo shipping contracts[48] and the same action was taken, soon thereafter, by the Department of Agriculture and the CCC. However, in all fairness to the navy's and other agencies' positions, it must be understood that elimination of the clause may not have enabled any vessel to enter a port otherwise barred to it.

On February 27, 1975, the CCC once again was shown to be an unwilling partner to a Boycott activity. Theodore J. Becker, controller of the CCC, confirmed that it held a 6.5 percent interest, totaling $11 million, in the Intra Investment Company of Beirut. Intra admittedly has been among the vanguard of Arab financial concerns blacklisting Western banks that deal with Israel. Originally, the CCC acquired $22 million in shares in a private bank that had failed and had been taken over by Intra. Thereafter, the CCC reduced its interest by half and has attempted, unsuccessfully, to sell its shares to the Lebanese government.[49]

Other Boycott actions, as well, have directly affected foreign governments. In 1953, the first joint Boycott action against a country, as such, was taken by the Arab League Council. In their conferences of November 1951 and August 1952, the regional Boycott offices attacked Cyprus as an entrepot from which

Israeli goods were transshipped to Arab states (and vice versa) on Cypriot manifests.[50] In 1953, the council "restricted imports of Cypriot products to those not duplicated in Israel . . . and exports to Cyprus . . . to the products which Cyprus normally consumed and which were not needed in Israel."[51] Although these rules, understandably, have been circumvented and, too, somewhat relaxed, Cypriot imports still are inspected carefully and several Cypriot firms have been boycotted by the Arab states for many years.

In 1960, Ceylon came under the attack of the Central Boycott Office. With Syria taking the initial action, the importation of all Ceylonese goods was banned because of the accreditation of the Ceylonese envoy to Israel.[52] A year earlier, in 1959, Arab delegations from the United Arab Republic (then Egypt and Syria), Algeria, Lebanon, and Morocco agreed to boycott the Yugoslav Trade Union Congress in protest against Israeli presence at the congress.[53] The Arabs also boycotted the Izmir Fair in 1955 due to Israel's participation.[54]

Finally, the Arab countries have resorted to diplomacy to extend the Boycott's effect. In June 1955, the director of the Arab Boycott visited the emirates of the Persian Gulf "in order to persuade their rulers to join the boycott of Israel."[55] Needless to say, the Boycott was successfully persuasive in this instance. Two months later, Radio Ramalla reported that the Iraqi government proposed "combined diplomatic action in certain European states in order to persuade them to disallow the citrus imports from Israel."[56] This proposal proved to be singularly unsuccessful. The Arab League Council also attempted, without success, to use diplomacy "in order to put an end to Israel's activities in Burma . . . as whatever strengthens Israel commercially, encourages her aggression against the Arabs.[57]

More recently, with the mercurial rise in Arab power due to the 1973-74 oil embargo and the consequent increase in oil prices, Arab diplomacy has proven more effective in assisting the Arab Boycott. Although the Boycott's rules and standards have remained constant, the Arab world has become a coveted market in the eyes of businessmen and industrialists. In order to cultivate the Arab market, these individuals "establish their own boycott rules which are much tighter than the official boycott. To be on the safe side they lean far over to be friendly to Arabs even if this means being overtly unfriendly to Israel."[58]

Yet, when the Arab Boycott confronts the giant American corporations, having their main interests outside the Arab world, it almost invariably meets its equal. On April 7, 1966, the Coca Cola Export Corporation refused a franchise to the Tempo Soft Drinks Company, Ltd., the largest Israeli bottling concern. The American corporation suggested that its decision to issue franchises was based solely on the following criteria: (1) that the arrangement be mutually profitable; (2) that the franchise applicant show a minimum million dollar investment; and (3) that the applicant give priority to the production and sale of Coca Cola as against any of its other soft drink brands.[59] These criteria, according to Coca Cola, were not met by Tempo.

However, the Anti-Defamation League, asked by Tempo to make an intensive investigation of the matter, reported that, in actuality, these prerequisites had been established only with respect to Israel:

> With respect to market feasibility, comparison studies of market conditions in Israel and its franchised neighboring countries ... revealed a vastly better market potential per capita in Israel. ...
> With respect to the minimum investment requirements, ... [in] El Salvador, for example, a country with a population roughly the same as Israel's, Coca Cola issued a franchise to a bottler whose operations began in 1965 with a capitalization of only $200,000. ... Of ten companies in eight comparable or neighboring countries ... the average investment came to about $245,000. The financial reports of the Tempo Company showed a total worth—including its new bottlemaking plant—of just under $3,000,000. Dun and Bradstreet rated the company's net worth—without the bottlemaking facility—at about half a million dollars.
> With respect to the [third] requirement ..., almost without exception, new franchise winners outside of Israel were, like Tempo, already in the business of manufacturing other brands of soft drinks as their primary product. Tempo, on the other hand, had offered to change the name of its company to "Coca Cola of Israel."[60]

Shortly thereafter, James A. Farley, chairman of the board of the Coca Cola Export Corporation, expressed two new reasons why the franchise had been denied. In past years, Coca Cola had approved an Israeli franchise application only to have Israel's government refuse to issue a permit to begin operations.[61] Moreover, in 1963, an Israeli court had found Tempo guilty of infringing Coca Cola's trademark and bottle design.[62]

Both explanations were refuted by the ADL report and by Moshe Bornstein, the managing director of Tempo. No permit, in fact, had ever been refused to a Coca Cola franchise holder. Farley's reference was probably to a 1950 franchise application by an American businessman that was soon withdrawn due to Israel's need, at that time, "of imports more basic than soda pop."[63] As for the infringement case, Bornstein stated that the case was settled out of court, with Tempo agreeing to use the name Tempo Kola instead of Tempo Cola. He added that the shape of the bottle was not at issue. Also, he maintained that Tempo agreed to the settlement only in order to maintain friendly relations with Cola Cola, with which Tempo was in the midst of negotiations for a franchise. Bornstein contended that, during the course of the three years of negotiations, the court action was not mentioned once.[64]

Coca Cola's decision created an uproar amongst American Jewry. On April 14, 1966, the ADL's Arnold Forster told the New York *Times* that he was "entirely opposed to suggestions that Jews in ... [the United States] refuse to purchase or sell Coca Cola [since] ... we entirely disapprove of the principle of Boycott."[65] However, many rabbis suggested that their congregants drink Pepsi

Cola and counter-Boycott threats were evinced by the Jewish War Veterans and other groups. Due to one of the shortest, most caustic and successful lobbying campaigns of this century, Coca Cola was forced to reverse its decision and, on April 15, 1966, granted a franchise to Abraham Feinberg, president of the Israeli Development Corporation (thereby entirely bypassing Tempo).[66]

Immediately, the Arab Boycott Committee gave Coca Cola three months to "clarify" its concessions arrangements, suggestively mentioning that more people drink Coke in Arab countries than in the United States itself.[67] Six months later, on November 20, 1966, the Arab League Boycott Conference in Kuwait voted unanimously for a ban by all Arab countries on dealings with Coca Cola, yet added that the "application of the ban is up to each member state of the Arab League."[68] It is ironic that the day before the conference opened, a Coca Cola advertisement appeared in *Al Ahram* announcing the opening of its new Kuwait plant. The situation was convoluted a bit further by Coca Cola's advertisements in *Al Ahram* for weeks prior to, and following, the conference, stressing the quality of its product and its contribution to Arab welfare and employment.[69]

Before describing the Boycott's present position in relation to Coca Cola, it is of interest to view the vicissitudes facing the Ford Motor Company, General Motors, and the Radio Corporation of America (RCA) during this same period. The conference in Kuwait blacklisted Ford on the same day that it banned Coca Cola. The reason offered was that Ford had entered into a licensing agreement, authorizing an Israeli concern, the Palestine Automobile Corporation, Ltd., to assemble British and American Ford trucks and tractors for the Israeli market, thereby reducing Israeli import duties on the finished product. The same conference was prepared to discuss the purported building of a General Motors assembly plant in Israel,[70] yet, just before the conference opened, General Motors issued a denial on the matter and its case was dropped.[71]

Ford warned the Arab governments that a boycott of its plants would not only put many agents out of work but would deprive at least 6,000 Arabs of jobs.[72] A similar warning was issued by the blacklisted RCA, claiming that such action would upset the Cairo television industry since television sets were assembled by a government-owned company principally from imported components manufactured by RCA ($3.5 million worth of parts were imported in 1965).[73]

On November 24, 1966, the New York *Times* reported that the Ford plant in the United Arab Republic (Egypt) had been seized by customs authorities. The alleged reason was that Ford owed $1.84 million in taxes on cars assembled at the plant or on their components. This was due to the Egyptian customs officials' claim that customs duties had to be paid on the entire car, even on such locally supplied items as tires, batteries, and upholstery. Ford had been negotiating this matter for the last eighteen months. The New York *Times* report added that 300 Egyptians had been put out of work by the Ford shut-down.[74]

The United Arab Republic's embassy in Washington, D.C., denied the seizure and said that the false accusation was "an attempt to confuse the issue and to cover Zionist embarrassment after the U.N. Security Council censure of Israeli aggression."[75] The embassy added that the customs duty dispute with Ford was not in any way influenced by the Boycott's decision. On the same day, sources in the U.S. Department of State agreed that, in fact, the Ford plant in Egypt had not been seized.[76] However, Ford's bank accounts in Egypt, containing $1.6 million, were confiscated by Egyptian officials and were later released only in return for a million dollar bank guarantee for payment of the customs duties.[77]

The Coca Cola and Ford cases merged at this juncture. Arab merchants received instructions to prevent the importation of the blacklisted companies' products. Yet, Coca Cola and Ford officials appeared nonplused since their plants were equipped with sufficient supplies and spare parts to last for the next two years.[78]

On December 13, 1966, the Middle East nations, realizing the important economic consequence of the Boycott's decision, announced that they would allow Arab plants to package and/or assemble and sell existing stocks of Coca Cola, Ford automobiles, and RCA appliances for the next nine months in order to minimize the disruptive effects of the blacklisting in the Arab business world. Again, they stressed the fact that the blacklisting was "not formally binding on the participating nations."[79]

With one exception, no ostensible move has been taken by individual Arab countries against the jumbo corporations since that time. In fact, despite being officially boycotted by the Arabs for dealing with Israel, Ford was asked, in early 1975, to build an automobile assembly plant in Syria.[80] The one exception was in Kuwait where, in February 1967, the government gave Coca Cola nine months to liquidate its interests in Kuwait and, because Ford was on the blacklist, asked Chrysler International's dealer in Kuwait to fill the country's $15 million demand for 1967 cars and trucks.[81]

Another example of a case in which American Jewish outrage helped offset the Arab Boycott's pressure against a large corporation involved the American Express Company. In their 1958 *Report on the Arab Boycott Against Americans,* the presidents of the seventeen major Jewish organizations in the United States mentioned, inter alia, that American Express had succumbed to Boycott pressures. In June 1958, due to the immediate publicity given to this report by the Anti-Defamation League and other organizations, a meeting of the Israel Government Tourist Corporation and representatives of the American Express Company was held in Jerusalem. There emanated from this meeting a joint statement announcing that American Express would undertake to reorganize and improve its representation in Israel. Its agencies will be enlarged and modernized in order to provide full range of services to an increased number of both local and foreign customers. . . . The joint promotion campaign . . . will stress both the traditional values of Israel as the Land of the Bible and the new sun and sea vacation attractions which are being developed in Israel.[82]

Even a major oil company, when confronted with public protest against its pro-Boycott policy, has retreated somewhat from its established policy. In January 1971, Israel revealed that a London-based subsidiary of Mobil Oil Company had ordered ship chandlers not to supply its tankers with Israeli goods because Libya had threatened to blacklist ships found with such supplies aboard. Although Mobil headquarters in New York later ordered that the directive be withdrawn, 1,457 Mobil credit cards were cancelled by customers. Of that number, 611 were renewed after Mobil conferred with American Jewish leaders and advertised in Jewish publications that "there is no Mobil boycott. There never was."[83]

As of January 1964, 164 U.S. firms,[84] along with about 500 foreign firms, were on the Arab Boycott's blacklist. In 1970, the U.S. companies on the blacklist climbed to approximately 1,500.[85] In addition to Ford, RCA, and Coca Cola, such industrial giants as Xerox, Zenith, Converse Rubber Company, American Biltrite, General Tire and Rubber Company, and Miles Laboratories appear on the blacklist.[86]

We have seen that the Boycott's effectiveness has varied with each situation. The cases of Coca Cola, Ford, RCA, and American Express illustrate the Boycott's major weakness. However, one must not minimize the Boycott's success. Further examples of, and statistical data on, its accomplishments will be presented in the following section.

POLITICAL, ECONOMIC, AND PSYCHOLOGICAL SUCCESSES

Proponents of Israel's cause often offer the argument that, since the Israeli economy has expanded rapidly since 1950, the Arab Boycott has been a total failure. The argument is presented by Frank Gervasi as follows:

Since 1950, Israel has enjoyed an economic growth rate of 10% annually, one of the world's highest; annual per capita income is $1,000 . . . and gross national product has outstripped population growth by 2.38 to 1, an unusually good performance in comparison with other developing nations. Israel's imports have increased from $423,106,000 in 1958 to $826,233,000 in 1964, and exports have risen in the same period from $139,102,000 to $351,821,000. . . . [Thus,] far from "strangling" Israel, the boycott actually may have stimulated the country's economic development by promoting greater self-reliance.[87]

This proposition was refuted in an article written in 1960 by Oded Remba:

[B]oycott or no boycott, Israel would have pressed the development of . . . [all] sectors of its economy, and this development would have been more favorable without the immense irritant of a blockade.[88]

Thus, we find even Gervasi admitting that "few Israelis would regret exchanging the Boycott for a more sensible economic stimulus: the free exchange of goods with all Arab neighbors."[89] Since the 1960s, the Boycott's success has been highlighted by its presence as an issue and a negotiating point in the Middle East peace negotiations.

The exact monetary effect of the Boycott on Israel's economy is uncertain. This is due to the impossibility of estimating the economic activity that would result were the Boycott rendered inoperative. The few estimates offered suggest that, until 1956, Israel was losing about $40 million per year because of Boycott pressures[90] while in the 1960s the annual loss estimates range from $10 million to $60-$70 million.[91] As a result of the introduction of oil as a political and economic weapon in the world arena, the Boycott's effectiveness has increased markedly. Its cost to Israel in the 1970s cannot be estimated at the present time.

The economic ramifications of the Boycott, vis-a-vis Israel, are manifold. The Arab efforts have adversely affected investments in, and trade with, Israel; impeded logical Middle East trade relations between Israel and the Arabs, thereby endangering Israel's economic security; prohibited transit of people and goods; and deterred tourist trade.[92] Furthermore, in the field of know-how, Israel has reached the stage where the know-how it needs is becoming more and more sophisticated and often concentrated in the hands of one or two large companies. Inasmuch as it is easier for the Arabs to pressure one or two, rather than a multitude of companies, Israel, hereafter, may face difficulties.[93]

There is a psychological impact, as well, resulting from the Arab economic activity. An atmosphere of fears and taboos, along with a shroud of uncertainty, has forced many companies to withdraw from all contacts with Israel.[94] The Arab Boycott threat, as well as the lack of security before the June war of 1967, has kept Western shipping lines from using the Eilat port.[95] Several British companies, such as British Leyland Motors, Ltd., have closed their offices in Israel or have withdrawn agencies from Israeli companies. "Some British firms are even refusing to import Israeli products or export to the country lest they get on the wrong side of the Arab fence."[96]

It is of interest to view some of Israel's losses, due to the energies of the Arab League, through the eyes of the journalist Marwan Iskandar:

> Oil has accounted for 10% of Israel's imports over the last 10 years.
> ... Had Iraqi and Saudi oil been allowed to come in, the pressures
> on the country's balance of payments would have been reduced
> appreciably. ...
>
> As a distorting factor, the boycott caused projects to be under-
> taken ... in Israel which would not have been economically justified
> in the absence of a boycott. The Eilat-Haifa pipeline ... is a clear
> example of distorted investment. ...
>
> In the absence of [a] boycott, ... Israel would seriously com-
> pete with Lebanon for international air traffic. ... The Israelis
> maintain a high standard in [the] ... field [of medical services and
> centers] and would compete with the Lebanese were it not for the
> boycott.[97]

We will see later, however, that Iskandar has observed that the Boycott's effects
have been far from one-sided.

The Boycott's ominous question to foreign business interests is, Why risk a
market of approximately 100 million Arabs for one of three million Israelis? The
Israeli government's answer is that the buying power of the population is more
important than its numerical size. This argument was of some persuasion prior to
1973. Israel's per capita income, in 1966, was about eight times higher than
that of the average Arab, and, in 1963, the imports to Israel "were exactly
33% of the combined imports of Egypt, Syria, Jordan, Iraq, Libya, Kuwait and
Saudi Arabia. ... [Also, if we] deduct both imports from Communist countries
and those from American surplus, the ratio rises to 2:3."[98] The 33 percent figure cited above is questionable and the proposed deduction rather arbitrary. Yet,
even granting all that is propounded above, a businessman, especially in the post-
bellum 1973 period, will find the following statement difficult to fully disregard:

> The Arabs are important consumers. ... Whatever they do not
> import from Israel, they have to import from other countries. When
> Israel tries to induce other countries to help in breaking the Arab
> boycott, it simply aims to acquire for itself these Arab markets. ...
> Remember, therefore, that Israel is the only loser [if the Boycott
> continues] and that it can recover this loss *only at your* expense.
> ...
>
> The Arabs possess a wide market which is being unified. ...
> They offer you good prospects of business and investment. They
> expect not only understanding but also cooperation in this legiti-
> mate and purely defensive measure of theirs, and it is definitely in
> your interest to cooperate.[99]

One company that was clearly convinced by this statement, even prior
to the October 1973 war, was Renault. This French government-owned manufacturer entered into an agreement with Kaiser-Frazer of Israel to supply

parts for the assembling of 2,400 units in Israel during an eighteen-month period. In August 1959, after about 800 units had been assembled, Renault abrogated the contract in response to pressure from the Arab Boycott. Attempts by France and Israel to reestablish the relationship failed and, in January 1960, Kaiser-Frazer brought breach of contract proceedings in the French courts for $1,872,700 in damages. Eventually, the case was settled out of court for $1 million.[100]

Soon thereafter, Renault agreed to construct an assembly plant in Cairo, with the hope of selling about 17,000 automobiles in the Arab countries every year. Subsequently, Renault's American sales, at least in part due to the company's seeming capitulation to the Boycott, dropped substantially. When it realized that its Cairo venture would not be as successful as expected, Renault attempted to reenter Israel's market but was rebuffed.[101] Thus, the Renault affair resulted in a pyrrhic victory for the Arabs and an economic disaster for the French company.[102]

An earlier example of a foreign company which was persuaded by the economic argument quoted above involved the English-owned British-American Tobacco Company, and its subsidiary, the Brown and Williamson Tobacco Company. Outside the continental United States, Alaska, and Hawaii, the British-American Tobacco Company has the right to market cigarettes under the names Pall Mall and Lucky Strike. (It should be noted that these brands have absolutely no connection with cigarettes of the same name marketed in the United States by a totally separate firm, the American Tobacco Company.) Brown and Williamson, acting as agent for the British-American Tobacco Company, manufactures and exports these cigarettes to foreign markets for its parent company.[103]

In March and April 1956, Brown and Williamson refused to fill orders by Israeli importers for Lucky Strike and Pall Mall. British-American Tobacco also refused Israeli orders for Senior Service cigarettes. In neither case was any explanation for the refusals offered. At about the same time, British-American Tobacco closed down a cigarette manufacturing company in Israel called Maspero. Although British-American Tobacco maintained that Maspero had been closed due to domestic and financial problems this contention could not be substantiated.[104]

It soon became clear that the motivation behind this unexplained policy was Arab pressure. In 1956 Duncan Oppenheim, chairman of the board of British-American Tobacco, admitted that the Arab League countries were "by far a better customer than Israel."[105] An additional factor behind British-American Tobacco's surrender to Arab demands was the fear that its large plant in Egypt (the Eastern Company) might be confiscated. Even after this plant had been expropriated, in October 1956, no move was made to restore Israeli trade relations, perhaps because British-American Tobacco still entertained hopes of recovering the plant.[106]

Brown and Williamson repeatedly attempted to shift responsibility for the tobacco company's policy toward Israel from itself to the parent company. However, the Anti-Defamation League continued to stress that, in essence, both companies were one, with only "technical, corporate separateness."[107] In a further effort to improve its image, British-American Tobacco spent hundreds of thousands of dollars in advertising in Jewish and Anglo-Jewish publications.[108]

Shortly thereafter, Brown and Williamson offered to sell Viceroy, Kool, and Raleigh brand cigarettes (three brands manufactured by Brown and Williamson for sale in the United States) to Israel with its parent company's consent. Its motives were not completely clear. Perhaps British-American Tobacco wanted to help perpetuate the notion of a separation between itself and Brown and Williamson for the sake of better public relations, or perhaps this policy was agreed upon in an effort to protect Brown and Williamson's American Jewish market. In any event, Israel refused the offer. Although the general counsel for Brown and Williamson, explained the refusal on the grounds that the Israeli government had blocked dollar payments on "non-essential items," Israel maintained that its real reason for refusing Brown and Williamson's offer was that as "long as the general boycott was in effect, Israel would not accept the . . . less popular brands offered."[109] Evidence, too, tended to contradict Yeamon's explanation since, in 1957, "Israel imported 10-12 million foreign cigarettes (80% from the United States, 20% from Great Britain) for local consumption, and about three times as many for the provision of its [commercial] ships and planes."[110]

No resolution of the tobacco case has taken place. The fact that British-American Tobacco yielded to Arab Boycott pressures may, at first glance, seem to refute the contention that large corporations are immune to Boycott demands. However, in fact, this case represents the exception that proves the rule. The British-American Tobacco Company, being a foreign corporation was, like Renault, better able to blunt the uproar created in the American Jewish community. Moreover, and in this instance unlike Renault, it was able to obfuscate, through its subsidiary's offer to sell cigarette brands to Israel, its true relationship to the Arab Boycott.

In any event, it should be recognized that this example occurred in the late 1950s and represents the first time in which the world was confronted with a major corporation's refusal to sell goods to Israeli importers.[111] As we have seen, in the 1960s, major firms such as Coca Cola, Ford, and RCA withstood, at the urging and with the support of a concerted and unified public, the pressures of the Arab Boycott. Later, Volkswagen rejected Arab efforts to force it to cancel all relations with Israel, notwithstanding the Arab threats to boycott the company's automotive products.[112]

An example of the Boycott's success, unparalleled during its thirty-year history, relates to Japan, most of whose businessmen have yielded to Arab economic pressures. One may find it difficult to understand why the Japanese have succumbed to the Boycott since, although Japan needs Arab oil, she is diversifying her sources of supply by dealing with Iran, the USSR, and China. Also, the Japanese have instituted exploration projects in Indonesia, Alaska, and the continental shelf of the Sea of Japan.[113] In addition, Japan's trade balance with the Arab countries is unfavorable. Japanese exports in 1966 to the Arab countries totaled nearly $300 million, while Japanese imports from these countries during the same period amounted to $850 million. In 1968, the export and import figures were $376 million and $1.1 billion, respectively. The major contribution to these negative trade balances of $550 million and $750 million was the importation of petroleum products.[114] Japan's total trade with Israel in 1968 was only $29 million.[115]

Another perplexity in the Japanese-Arab situation is that Japan's attentiveness to Middle East politics is not paralleled in her trade relations with the rest of the world: "Japan lives by her exports. The United States absorbs about one-third of these. The . . . member states of the Arab League absorb . . . 3 percent."[116] The fact that the United States is her biggest customer and supplier has not deterred Japan's attempts to expand her flourishing trade with mainland China, estimated at $600 million in 1966.[117] Thus, if "Japan's [trading] plans . . . are postulated on a progressive relaxation of both foreign and Japanese trade restrictions,"[118] one may question how Japan justifies its willingness to openly flout U.S. wishes by trading with Communist China and, at the same time, placate Arab demands by reducing its trade with Israel.

However, one must avoid viewing a large, industrialized nation's trade relations in terms of logic and reason. Since the end of World War II, the Japanese have been "chiefly concerned with immediate issues and have given little thought to the broad outlines of the world economy."[119] Hence, perhaps Japan's yielding to Arab Boycott threats should be regarded both as the "collective rationalization of the Ministry of International Trade and Industry and the big Japanese concerns, and [as] the independent rationalization of individual firms."[120] Such rationalizations give precedence to immediate, rather than long-term, monetary gain along with, perhaps, hopes for taking the Arab oil concessions away from the West. Hence, little importance is given to considerations of fair trade.

Admittedly, to say that Japanese firms have succumbed to the Boycott is a generalization. Matsushita (Panasonic trademark in the United States) and Hitachi, before 1965, agreed to do business with Israel, as long as the transactions were secret and indirect. When, in 1965, Israel announced that these firms, along with all other foreign firms, would have to trade openly with Israel or lose their import licenses, Matsushita announced that it would no longer permit its forty companies to comply with the Boycott. Meanwhile, Nissei Sangyo, Ltd., a subsidiary of Hitachi which manufactures televisions, radios, and appliances, informed the Anti-Defamation League that it never had a policy of discriminating against Israel and added that it was "willing to do business there as well as in other countries through agents or trading companies."[121] In addition, the Fuji Photo Company announced that it would no longer capitulate to Boycott pressures and promptly participated, along with forty other Japanese firms,[122] in Japan's pavilion at the 1968 Tel Aviv International Trade Fair.[123] Fuji's name appears on the 1970 blacklist.[124]

However, many major Japanese firms openly comply with the Boycott. These include Sumitomo, Mitsubishi, Mitsui, Suzuki, Nippon Electric, Shiba Electric, Japan Air Lines (JAL), Nissan Motor Company (Datsun), and Toyota. The last three companies' capitulation to the dictates of the Boycott is reflected by the following actions and statements: (1) JAL has refused to enter into a mutual landing agreement with El Al;[125] (2) in 1969, Datsun announced that its export of 20,000 units a year to the Arab countries would be jeopardized by establishing a trade link with Israel;[126] and (3) Toyota has claimed that it "could not increase its sales outlets without sacrificing the requirements of old distributors and dealers," despite reports to the contrary in the October 27, 1969 edition of *U.S. News and World Report.*[127] In April 1970, Lawrence Peirez, chairman of the Anti-Defamation League's fact-finding committee, and Forster went to Tokyo to meet with officials of these companies.[128] These private meetings, in the main, were unsuccessful and ultimately resulted in the release of the facts cited above to the international press. Although public denials ensued, no change in the policies of these corporations has taken place (as discussed below with regard to JAL).

Another example of a Japanese corporation complying with the Boycott regulations involves the shipper Marubeni-Iida. Although Marubeni-Iida agreed after 1965 to use Israel's Zim and Elyam lines for shipping, on September 19, 1968, Avner Manor, president of the American-Israeli Shipping Company, alleged that the Japanese shipper had reneged on its agreement. As proof he presented the following incidents:

> 1) A 10,000 ton shipment of coal was loaded on ZIM's m/v *Beer-sheva* at Hampton Roads, Virginia, for discharge in Japan. Marubeni-Iida telexed: "Sorry cannot entertain Israeli flag."
> 2) Two bales of raw silk, weighing 308 lbs., were loaded at Newark for Kobe on ZIM's m/v *Deganya,* which is operated by Pacific Star Lines. Marubeni-Iida's bank ordered the shipper to stop, discharge the load, and not use Pacific Star Line vessels.[129]

On August 5, 1974, the Boycott's office in Damascus announced that the Sony Corporation had been placed on the blacklist for dealing with Israel. According to the Boycott aide who made the announcement, Sony, which manufactures electronic equipment and has substantial investments in Arab countries, in mid-1973 failed to reply to a Boycott warning to stop dealing with Israel.[130]

In late February 1975, Boycott Commissioner General Mohammed Mahgoub announced that Sony's name would be lifted from the Boycott blacklist as soon as it concluded pending agreements with Arab countries.[131] Although this Boycott action strongly indicates that Sony, henceforth, will comply with Boycott regulations relating to trade with Israel, one must recall that many large corporations, such as IBM, are not on the blacklist and yet do business with both Israel and the Arab countries. Thus, it will be of interest to observe Sony's future economic relations with Israel.

The Japanese government has attempted to refute the accusations regarding its association with the Arab Boycott's policies. It contends that its policy is to develop trade with all countries and allow Japanese companies to make their own decisions. With regard to its decision not to participate in the International Trade Fair, held in Tel Aviv in June 1968, the decision allegedly was made on budgetary and economic, not political, grounds.[132] (See Appendix C for letters from Japanese firms to Israeli companies regarding Japanese-American trade.)

In order to mollify Israel, Shaie Jurandhi, Japanese deputy foreign minister for parliamentary affairs, visited Israel in June 1968, and issued a joint communique with the Israeli government. The communique was noted in the Israeli newspaper *Haaretz* as follows: "[T]he two governments favor increased economic, technical and cultural cooperation between the two countries. The two governments agreed that a political interference in normal trade relations should not be permitted."[133]

However, Japan's reaction to the Boycott, in contrast to the reactions of many other countries (to be shown later), has been one of pronouncements rather than deeds. In December 1972, the ADL issued a summary of Israel's negotiations with Japan and JAL regarding the proposed mutual air agreement between El Al and JAL. Over the course of a five-year period, it became clear that the Japanese government, in concert with JAL, sought to depict an open-minded attitude toward the negotiations while, in fact, never intending to enter into such an arrangement due to the pressures emanating from the Boycott Office. Although JAL insisted that "we fly for profit and not for protocol," it rejected El Al's proposal to fly between Tel Aviv and Tokyo and share the profits with JAL, without an obligation on the part of JAL to reciprocate in terms of committing planes or flight schedules to Israel.[134]

From the above, the ADL concluded that the negotiations had been conducted in bad faith and, on December 4, 1972, advertised in the New York *Times* that "Japan Air Lines has joined the Arab Boycott against Israel: Let's do something about it." Since that time, memoranda have been circulated in Jewish communities throughout the United States urging people not to fly on JAL and, in 1972 and 1973, pickets appeared in front of JAL headquarters in New York.[135]

GAPS, SHORTCOMINGS, AND FAILURES

As we have seen, the main goal of the Arab League's Boycott is the "economic strangulation" of the State of Israel.[136] This being its purpose, surely one must conclude that the Boycott has been a partial success. A lesser view of the Boycott's success was taken by Alfred Lilienthal, counsel for the American-Arab Association for Commerce and Industry in the United States, and an ardent anti-Zionist, who observed that the Boycott had been "a real flop."[137]

The Boycott's supporters offer three economic developments in Israel as proof that the Boycott has been effective: Israel's rising cost of living; the repeated devaluations of the Israeli pound; and Israel's unfavorable balance of payments due to an excess of imports over exports. However, the cause-and-effect relationship between the Arab Boycott and Israel's economic problems is difficult to accept. It is arguable that these developments have merely been a sign of Israel's rapid rate of growth.[138]

Before the enormous increase in oil income, although the Arabs' efforts may have resulted in a loss of $60-$70 million each year for Israel's economy, one was forced to recognize the validity of Gervasi's argument that Israel's economy had flourished nonetheless while those of the Arab countries, although expanding, had not approached Israel's growth rate. Since 1960, Israel's exports had doubled, and the country had formed ties with twenty-eight countries in Europe, twenty-nine in Africa, all twenty-six countries in the Western Hemisphere, and fourteen countries in Asia and Oceania.[139] Israel's market, although not as large as that of the Arabs, was "by no means negligible."[140]

In addition, there was something to say for the contention that the Arab economic pressure, more often than not, helped the cause of national unity and, hence, that of Israel's survival. Due to its inability to purchase Egyptian cotton, Israel grew its own cotton. When Israel realized that it would be forced to trade far from its natural markets, it developed a large merchant marine (more than 1.5 million tons in 1971 compared to 22,000 in 1948). Moreover, given the initial unwillingness on the part of some airlines to land in Israel, El Al was formed and has flourished.[141]

There were, and are, many other reasons for Israel's ability to substantially overcome the Boycott's activities. Israel receives in excess of $1.5 billion every year from foreign sources such as German restitutions, contributions of world Jewry, and capital investments. Also, Iran, on the whole, has ignored the Boycott, thereby giving Israel a large portion of its much needed oil supply.

Of greater importance for the future appeared to be the African market south of the Sahara. Prior to the 1973 war, Israel was in a position to act as a large-scale contractor, advisor, and supplier of technical aid and, despite the Arab League's protestations, "most African countries continue[d] to prefer their material interests to any ideological considerations."[142] Actually, it was the Boycott, itself, that forced Israel into its policy of presence in Africa and Asia, and this, in turn, created new sympathies for Israel's cause.[143]

An overly optimistic picture of the above thought was presented in 1960 by a French political economist, Ernest Teilhac:

The boycott of Israel is a double-edged weapon. Undoubtedly, it
deprives Israel of economic interaction with its nearest neighbors,
but at the same time, it allows [Israel] to substitute other economic
relations, not only with the United States and Europe but with
Africa and the Far East as well. An economic boundary is not geo-
graphic. Thus Israel is free to establish one, thanks to an external
monetary agreement, which for Israel, too, would not be truly
external. One must never forget that Israel is not only in Israel
itself. One must never forget that under the superficial restraints of
an economy under seige [there exists] the broad structure of a
mixed economy.[144]

With the opening of the Gulf of Aqaba to Israel shipping in 1956, Israel
was able to expand its trade with the Afro-Asian nations and to offset, to some
extent, the Suez ban on shipping and cargoes. By 1970 the Histadrut construction enterprise, Solel Boneh, alone, had won contracts valued at $40 million in
nine African countries. The Cairo daily newspaper, *Al Akhbar*, in that same
year, warned that

Israel's infiltration into the new states . . . is a means to break this
blockade and to reduce its effect. If Israel succeeds in bolstering its
relations with these states and these peoples, it would find a way to
undermine our boycott. Thus we would have a useless and ineffective measure against Israel.[145]

At the time, the Eilat port only handled 3 percent of Israel's total export
volume, and hope for a *concours exterieur de capitaux* was highly improbable.
Yet, prior to the Yom Kippur war, one could not discount the potential of the
African market and its importance to Israel's goal of circumventing the Arab
Boycott. Evidence of the budding relationship between Israel and the African
nations appeared in 1964 when Israel was granted full membership in the Afro-
Asian bloc of the UN Trade Conference.[146] Certainly, Egypt seemed to have
taken this threat seriously. In 1965, it began distributing pamphlets in English-
speaking areas of Africa entitled "Israel, the Enemy of Africa."[147]

Of course, Israel's hopes regarding Africa have been dashed, at least
temporarily, due to the Arab economic power resulting from the 1973-74 oil
crisis. With the exception of three small countries, all African nations have
broken off diplomatic relations with Israel. Since Idi Amin's sudden reversal of
policy in Uganda in 1972, many Israeli contractors have been asked to leave
Africa and there is a consensus that much of the African market must be dis-
counted at least for the 1970s. Yet, the Arab Boycott can take no credit for
Israel's present problems in Africa. In fact, the present adverse situation exists
in spite of the Boycott's activities which initially caused Israel to seek and win
the African market.

In addition to the existence of alternate world markets and suppliers, the defiance by large corporations has been another vitiating influence upon the Boycott's success. We have already seen how Coca Cola, RCA, and Ford, although blacklisted, have yet to be seriously harmed because of their dealings with Israel. Other large American corporations defying Boycott regulations have been American Biltrite, Converse Rubber Company, General Tire and Rubber Company, Twentieth Century Fox, International Telephone and Telegraph, Music Corporation of America, General Motors, Chrysler, the Sheraton Hotel Corporation, and the Hilton Hotel Corporation.[148] In Hilton's case, Conrad Hilton refused to submit to the Boycott because it was "counter to the principles we live by," yet the Boycott Committee decided that because "Hilton's interests were in managing hotels rather than owning them, it did not violate the fundamental intent of the boycott,"[149] since "the remitted fees weaken Israel's balance of payments."[150] The Boycott appears to discount the fact that good hotels attract money-spending tourists.

One of the worst setbacks that the Boycott ever experienced was with regard to the Chase Manhattan Bank. On July 10, 1964, the Arabs announced that they would boycott Chase because the bank was the transfer agent for Israel Bonds.[151] Chase was given a six-month period in which to terminate its affairs in Israel while the Arab countries were given the same six months in which to settle their vast financial affairs with the bank.[152] This declaration by Mohammed Mahgoub in Damascus was strongly supported by only one country—Syria.[153] Egypt, in fact, opposed such a move since it already had received $10 million in credit from Chase Manhattan.[154] Mahgoub attempted to pressure the bank by announcing that Kuwait might withhold a $200 million deposit, yet Kuwait quickly denied this allegation.[155]

Finally, the Boycott Committee yielded to pressure from many of its members and, on January 4, 1965, announced that its ultimatum date had been cancelled because "certified documents" emphasized that the bank's relations with Israel were of "a purely banking nature."[156] To paraphrase, when the Arabs find a particular relationship beneficial, they will continue to deal with companies doing business with Israel.*

Mention should be made of public pronouncements relating to Chase Manhattan's refusal to open a branch in Israel. This refusal may indicate a partial subservience to the Boycott but there is a need to temper criticism of a bank which, as opposed to other banking institutions in the United States, has withstood previous Boycott pressures and has continued as the transfer

---

*In fact, the Boycott Office specifically excepts from the Boycott rules any international banking institutions from which the Arabs derive greater benefits than those derived by Israel notwithstanding the extent of the banks' relationships with Israel.

agent for Israel Bonds, an act which could have subjected Chase Manhattan to blacklisting The Exchange National Bank of Chicago (ENB) has been the only banking institution in the United States to open branches in Israel and it appears that the Chicago bank's decision was reached on the basis of social and cultural, rather than purely economic considerations. Eventually, ENB's branches in Israel were acquired by Bank Japhet and adopted a new name, American Israel Bank Ltd. (a member of the Bank Hapoalim group).[157]

Other examples of Arab reluctance to ban lucrative trade with foreign companies simply to meet the ideological objectives of the Boycott relate to West Germany and Romania. When the former was threatened with Arab recognition of East Germany and the loss of Arab business if it were to sign a reparation agreement is Israel, Bonn, nevertheless, proceeded to sign the agreement. The Arab countries, "needing the German market more than the Germans needed the Arab markets, looked the other way."[158] Germany also has resisted Arab pressure relating to loan syndications.[159]

In 1967, Romania agreed to increase its trade with Israel by 600 percent to $20 million by the end of 1968. This breach in the Arab Boycott did not bring about Arab retaliation,[160] nor did the subsequent airline and industrial agreements between the two countries.

With Boycott selectivity and flexibility being the rule at present, it is of interest to note the following Arab League regulations making it easier for the Arabs to live with their own Boycott:

1. International loan agencies, like the World Bank, will not be blacklisted for lending money to Israel if Arab countries also are members.

2. Arab states will no longer boycott the Mogen David, six-pointed star emblem, per se. However, goods bearing the emblem must be carefully checked and the supplying company must certify that the goods are not of Israeli origin.

3. Commercial banks will not be blacklisted for dealing with Israel if Arabs have statistical evidence that the bank has loaned more money to Arabs than to Israelis.

4. An Arab buying rights to a film before he has found out that its stars have "Zionist tendencies" will be allowed to show the film for six months so that he will not lose money.[161]

5. Egypt no longer will ask tourists their religion, and no longer will care what other Middle Eastern countries the tourists have visited previously.[162]

6. The Qatar Boycott Office advised that in case a foreign corporation feels that its chamber of commerce or notary public will refuse to endorse the negative certificate of origin (see Appendix A), the signature of any Arab embassy will be satisfactory. Also, "affirmative" certifications, stating that the goods are exclusively of U.S. (or another country's) origin, will be accepted in lieu of the "non-Israel certificate."[163]

Inconsistencies in applying the Boycott have plagued the Arab League from the outset. In theory, if a firm is on the Central Boycott Office list, it is on the list of every member. Yet, "many firms have been placed on the central list, but not on the national lists. Others have been on one or more national lists, but not on the central list."[164] In addition, where a firm is removed from the central blacklist in Damascus, it may or may not be deleted automatically from the country lists, and the reverse, likewise, is true. Thus,

> ... enforcement is not uniform from market to market. In general, Morocco, Algeria, Tunisia, [and] Sudan, ... do not let it [the Boycott] hinder their business activity. General Tire holds equity in factories in both Israel and Morocco, despite the fact that it is [black]listed. Morocco even ships some merchandise directly to Israel and allows blacklisted ships to use its ports. Recently, the French holiday-camp organization, Club Mediterranee, was blacklisted on account of its Israeli camp, although its successful Moroccan operation continues, perhaps because of the 20,000 tourists it attracts annually.[165]

Lebanon, too, has been accused of procrastination in implementing the Boycott.[166] In 1959 Lebanon permitted the importation of automobile spare parts, with the exception of chassis and engines, from boycotted firms if it was not able to obtain these parts from other sources. It seems that most Arab countries provide for such exceptions regarding spare parts and other necessities, "either by decree or by quietly ignoring the letter of the boycott action."[167]

Another example of this divergence in Arab views occurred in Jordan in 1963. The Helena Rubinstein cosmetic firm owns a manufacturing plant in Migdal Haemek, Israel. The company had been blacklisted for many years (its name appears twice on the blacklist, under different spellings). Yet, on April 30, 1963, in Amman, the Hashemite kingdom's radio station devoted an entire program to the late Mrs. Rubinstein, praising her person and products, and urging Jordanian women to follow her beauty suggestions.[168]

Petty quarrels, too, have plagued the Boycott apparatus. In January 1963, a dispute arose over the dismissal of the commissioner general of the Arab League Office for the Boycott of Israel. The commissioner was a Syrian, Abdal-Karim al-'Aidi, and the permanent headquarters were in Damascus. Al-'Aidi had held his post since 1950 but had incurred Cairo's displeasure in September 1962 by accepting certain documents from the Egyptian military attache in Beirut who had defected and taken asylum in Syria. Possibly acting upon pressure from the Egyptian government, the secretary general of the Arab League, 'Abd al-Khaliq Hassuna, relieved al-'Aidi of his post and appointed an Egyptian, Mahgoub, in his place. The Damascus government took this as a direct challenge and, with Jordanian, Saudi, and Iraqi support, refused to recognize the legality of Mahgoub's appointment. Therefore, it established a "regional" Boycott office in Damascus under its own authority, and contended that al-'Aidi could only be dismissed by the Arab League Council.[169] Although by way of a compromise, and due to the fact that the Syrian government was overthrown in March 1963 by a pro-Nasser group, Mahgoub is (at this writing) still commissioner general, a Lebanese journalist, writing of this incident, commented: "Israel can henceforth have the moral satisfaction of no longer being the country placed under the ban of the organization formed by her neighbors, but simply one of the countries of this region that boycott each other."[170]

Another feature of the Boycott which has tended to render it less effective is the tardy blacklisting of flagrant offenders of Boycott regulations. It took the Arabs two years to blacklist International Paper and Union Bag-Camp after their well-publicized $2.65 million joint investment in Israel in 1959. Also, shortly after Monsanto's Chemstrand Division, with much fanfare, began construction of an acrylic fiber plant in Israel in 1962, the parent corporation received a substantial order for an insecticide from Egypt. Only in 1964 did it receive the standard Boycott questionnaire.[171] Monsanto's name appears on the 1970 blacklist.[172]

Major blunders and absurdities, too, have beset the Arab League's boycott actions. Random examples follow:

1. According to the New York *Times,* 60 percent of all British companies on the blacklist in 1963 were not affected because they had no dealings with the Arabs in the first place.[173]

2. An Israeli ship, the *Nurith,* was sold in 1965 to a Greek corporation and renamed the *Kyriaki,* yet the Arabs announced that the ship would remain on the blacklist.[174]

3. In refusing to participate in international meetings or commissions with Israeli representatives, the Arabs have impeded the operations of the UN Locust Control Commission, and have rendered "ineffective the work of the Regional Council of the World Health Organization as well as other specialized agencies in the Middle East."[175]

4. An Egyptian corporation, the General Company for Trading and Chemicals, in 1966 sent a letter to the New York Coat and Suit Association, in the center of New York's garment district, whose membership was 85 percent Jewish. The letter asked if the association might want to export to the Egyptian market, provided that it would answer the Boycott questionnaire regarding its business connections with Israel. Actually, the association, one of the large contributors to the development of Israel's garment industry, provides no exporting nor production of its own.[176]

5. The Arabs have accused Israel of loading worthless goods on ships and sending these ships through the Suez Canal. Israel, according to an Arab source, hoped that these goods would be impounded, thereby enabling it to raise the matter before the United Nations.[177]

6. In 1965, the Arabs threatened to "boycott" Prince Philip because he had agreed to appear in Glasgow at a party "sponsored by the Women's International Zionist Organization and his favorite children's aid society, aboard a ferry being built for the Israeli Merchant Marine."[178]

7. In one Arab country, a Yale Glee Club recording was "blacklisted" because Hebrew writing was found on the Yale University seal.[179]

8. Jewish organizations such as Hadassah, ADL, and the American Committee for Bar-Ilan University, appear on the blacklist.[180]

9. The Bahai religious sect, due to the location of its world center in Haifa, Israel, has been blacklisted for engaging in propaganda discrediting the Arabs. The founder of the Bahai faith, Bah'u'llah, was exiled to what was then Palestine in 1868, when the land was under Ottoman rule, and established the sect's center and shrines in the neighboring cities of Haifa and Acre.[181]

However, as briefly noted earlier, perhaps the major factor leading to the Boycott's ineffectiveness has been the manner in which corporations have managed to circumvent its regulations. It is common knowledge that a bribe of $2,000 to $5,000 is often enough to have a name removed from the blacklist.[*] It is perhaps for this reason that leaders of Al Fatah have called the Arab Boycott Office "a sinecure for parasites and inefficient officials."[182]

Companies that have gone into Israel secretly have used a number of different methods:

> One is to license an Israeli company via a third, already boycotted, company, which then sub-licenses the Israeli firm. Another method is to license via a Yugoslav firm. More common is the handling of Israeli business through a separate division, affiliate, licensee, or subsidiary set up just for this purpose—with a name unrelated to that of the parent firm. . . . Some companies have even sent communications without letterhead, [with] unsigned designs, etc., to Israeli licensees.[183]

Even the blacklisted firms have been able to trade with Arab countries under the "official transactions" oasis. In theory, the Boycott is aimed only at commercial sales. Where a government purchasing office determines that a product found on the blacklist is superior to its nonblacklisted competitors,

---

[*]In early 1976, several blacklisted companies were told by senior Egyptian officials that they might be removed from the blacklist if they were to match their investments in Israel with investments in an Arab country. On this basis, four other Arab League countries have indicated a willingness to remove companies from the blacklist [*The Jerusalem Post* 9, no. 3 (February 18, 1976)].

it may proclaim a contract relating to such product to be an "official transaction."[184]

In addition, Boycott officials have devised other loopholes of their own. Sales to Israel of goods and services for other than military or economic development have been viewed "with delight" by these officials, on the premise that such transactions result in a drain on Israel's hard-currency reserves.[185] We have seen this reasoning in operation, previously, in the Hilton and Sheraton cases.

Similarly, although the aircraft manufacturing company owned and operated by Marcel Dassault has been blacklisted, Egypt asked France for 44 Mirage F-1s, joining Libya, Kuwait, Saudi Arabia, and Abu Dhabi as customers for Dassault aircraft. The following reason was given: "We buy our planes from France, not from Mr. Marcel Dassault."[186]

The general provisions barring all ships that have traded with Israel from calling at any Arab port have been evaded in the following ways: First, a special clause, added to foreign flagships' charters by an Egyptian company, states that "it is understood that the vessel has called at all ports of the Eastern Mediterranean and the Egyptian authorities have been duly advised of this. The Egyptian authorities guarantee that the vessel and her owners will not suffer any delay, difficulties, expenses and/or damages, direct or indirect, owing to such calls in all Eastern Mediterranean countries." Second, "universal tourism ships" have not been affected by Boycott activities.[187] Third, a modification in the Suez Canal regulations now permits ships that have traded with Israel to take on fuel and water in an emergency.[188] Thus, to a certain extent, one may say that the Arabs have left "major gaps through which the whole substance of blockade has somehow evaporated."[189]

On March 29, 1975, French syndicators of major loan transactions discovered a manner in which to circumvent the blacklisting of Jewish-controlled banks. A small group of banks will offer to purchase an entire issue of bonds to be marketed by a corporate borrower. Each bank in this group, without consulting other members, is then free to bring in other banks, which may include those on the blacklist, to assist in underwriting and distributing its share of the issue. Details relating to the manner in which syndicate profits or percentages are to be divided are presently being resolved.[190]

Finally, we must view the adverse economic effect* of the Boycott on its perpetrators, the Arab countries. Certainly, it precludes Israeli capital investment in the neighboring Arab states. Furthermore, it has created economic distortions in the Arab world:

---

*The international political effect of the Boycott upon the Arabs themselves will be seen in the next chapter.

Iraq's losses through its ceasing to pump oil through the Kirkuk-Haifa pipeline amounted to $150 million by 1955. . . .

Pipelines from Saudi Arabia to the Mediterranean were carried through Lebanon as a consequence of the boycott regulations, although it would have been cheaper to take them through Israel.

[In addition], the development of Aqaba port would not have been feasible if Jordan had access to Haifa or Jaffa.[191]

It is impossible to gauge the foreign investment and trade lost by the Arabs due to the Boycott's efforts. There are persuasive arguments that, prior to 1946, a substantial volume of trade existed between Palestine and the Arab states and, in the absence of the Arab Boycott, this trade would have been greatly expanded.[192]

Michael Shefer, an economist in the Israel Ministry of Finance, estimated in 1964 that, excluding oil, exports from five Arab countries (Egypt, Iraq, Jordan, Lebanon, and Syria) to Palestine amounted to about 5 percent of total Arab exports in 1938. By 1944, this figure was 18 percent, and in 1946, despite the commencement of the Boycott, total Arab exports to Palestine had remained the same, although the percentage figure dropped to 9 percent. With regard to these same five states' imports (but, this time, including oil) from Palestine, the figures were 1 percent in 1938, 8.5 percent in 1944, and 4.5 percent in 1946.[193]

Shefer also estimated that, in the absence of the Arab Boycott, the value of Israel's annual imports in 1964 from Arab states would have been approximately $120 million (mostly in manufactured goods, fuel, and raw material) while its exports to the Arab countries would have amounted to only $40 million.[194] Surely between 1964 and 1975 this imbalance would have been maintained. In view of this potential Arab balance of trade surplus, it is not surprising to find Marwan Iskandar write that "the boycott exercises an adverse effect on both Israel's economy and the economies of some Arab countries. . . ."[195] This ambivalent attitude received added support in June 1966 when Lebanon's minister of the interior, Pierre Gemayel, "called for a total revision of the boycott system and noted that negative action had shown itself to be barren of result."[196]

Even in the post-1973 Arab financial boom, there is every reason to believe that the Arab balance of trade surplus with Israel would remain. Although the Arab buying power has increased, Israel yearns to be able to substitute many Arab goods for those faraway, more expensive products of the West which it is forced to purchase.

It is difficult to assess the present effectiveness of the Boycott in its economic drive against Israel. The Boycott has received a great deal of publicity, which it must regard as its worst nemesis. Yet, what may prove ironic is that certain of the Boycott's goals will be achieved notwithstanding its own ineffectiveness, due to the nascent, yet booming, attraction of the Arab markets.

Countries and corporations, alike, are presently finding the financial lure of these markets irrepressible. Yet, questions remain. Will the Arab nations, through their Boycott, wealth, or a combination of both, succeed in persuading the world to cut off its trade with Israel? And even if the Arabs were successful in this regard, will their wealth and power be everlasting or evanescent? The world's myopia, which was evinced in the economic crisis of 1973-74, will redound to the Arabs' detriment if, and when, the Middle East oil boom begins to wane. The fickle decisional blade of the world's economic giants is double-edged and, just as quickly as the Arabs were "cut in," they may find themselves "cut out."

NOTES

1. "Arab-Israel Conflict and the United Nations," *International Review Service* 8, no. 73 (1962): 30. See also Abba Eban, *Voice of Israel* (New York: Horizon Press, 1957), p. 256.

2. Ibid.

3. Resolution S/2322, UN Security Council, September 1, 1951.

4. UN Document S/PV.664, verbatim record of the six-hundred sixty-fourth meeting of the Security Council, March 20, 1954, New York.

5. Frank Gervasi, *The Case for Israel* (New York: The Viking Press, 1967), p. 137.

6. Eban, op. cit., p. 260.

7. Jerusalem *Post*, November 13, 1975.

8. Jerusalem *Post*, November 14, 1975.

9. World Jewish Congress, *Evidence of the Arab War in Peacetime Against Israel* (Tel Aviv: Hadfus Haklali, 1957), p. 51.

10. *Daily News Bulletin* (Jewish Telegraph Agency), March 5, 1975, p. 2.

11. New York *Times*, March 4, 1975. The other eleven companies, some of which act as agents for foreign carriers, are F. W. Hartmann and Company, Inc.; Barber Steamship Lines, Inc.; States Marine-Isthmian Agency, Inc.; Crossocean Shipping Company, Inc.; Hellenic Lines, Ltd.; the Peralta Shipping Corporation; the Kerr Steamship Company, Inc.; Boise-Griffin Steamship Company, Inc.; Constellation Navigation, Inc.; the Central Gulf Steamship Corporation; and Nedlloyd, Inc.

12. United Nations, *Treaty Series* 15 (1948). See also Gervasi, op. cit., p. 132.

13. Washington *Evening Star*, September 30, 1965. See also Gervasi, op. cit., p. 132, and New York *Times*, October 15, 1957.

14. There were also allegations that Air France had produced "propaganda films" for Israel. Robert W. MacDonald, *The League of Arab States: A Study in the Dynamics of Regional Organization* (Princeton, N.J.: Princeton University Press, 1965), p. 120.

15. New York *Times*, March 18, 1957.

16. Oded Remba, "The Arab Boycott: A Study in Total Economic Warfare," *Midstream* 6, no. 3 (Summer 1960): 47.

17. New York *Times*, February 22, 1965.

18. New York *Times*, March 9, 1965, and March 23, 1963.

19. New York *Times*, December 22, 1963.

20. Abba Eban, "The Answer to Arab Boycott," in *The Israel Yearbook, 1966* (Jerusalem: Israel Yearbook Publications, Ltd., 1966), p. 20. See also *Facts* 16, no. 1 (January 1965): 298, and *Britain and Israel*, no. 41 (February 1975): 2.

21. World Jewish Congress, op. cit., p. 56.

22. New York *Times*, December 3, 1963.

23. Ibid.

24. New York *Times*, December 10, 1963.

25. New York *Times*, December 9, 1963.

26. New York *Times*, December 11, 1963.

27. New York *Times*, December 12, 1963.

28. New York *Times*, December 13, 1963.

29. New York *Times*, December 13, 1963.

30. Ibid.

31. Felix Kessler, "Knuckling Under," *The New Republic*, March 8, 1975.

32. "Several Arab countries include film censorship within the authority of the local Boycott Office, and the titles of banned films and performers appear in official boycott decrees. In other countries, the film censors are provided the boycott guidelines, and the local Boycott Offices are not involved." James H. Bahti, *The Arab Economic Boycott of Israel* (Washington, D.C.: The Brookings Institution, 1967), p. 11.

33. *Facts* (Anti-Defamation League) 12, no. 2, (March-April 1957): 101. See also *ADL Bulletin*, March 1960, p. 3.

34. New York *Times*, March 18, 1959.

35. New York *Times*, October 23, 1961.

36. *Near East Report* 9, no. 1 (January 12, 1965). See also New York *Times*, July 17, 1963.

37. New York *Times*, January 29, 1965.

38. New York *Times*, February 27, 1965.

39. New York *Times*, July 29, 1960. The Central Boycott Office has banned the importation into Arab markets of eggs, poultry, citrus fruits, plastics, and phonograph records from Iran, with a proviso that "the ban is to be imposed in accordance with the laws of each state." "General Principles for Boycott of Israel," Section 37(a).

40. New York *Times*, December 3, 1960, and December 26, 1960.

41. New York *Times*, December 15, 1963.

42. "Arab-Israel Conflict and the United Nations," *International Review Service*, op. cit.

43. U.S., *Treaties and Other International Acts Series*, no. 2290; and Gervasi, op. cit., p. 132. See also Washington *Evening Star*, September 30, 1956. Cf. *Foreign Commerce Weekly* (U.S. Department of Commerce), March 5, 1956; American Jewish Congress, *The Arab Campaign Against American Jews* (New York: 1956), pp. 33-34; and *ADL Bulletin*, October 1954, p. 3.

44. *ADL Bulletin*, October 1954, p. 3.

45. New York *Times*, March 28, 1964. This stipulation, in 1964, was held by a federal district court to be within the navy's rights.

46. New York *Times*, January 22, 1960. For the exact provisions of the military sea transportation policy, see New York *Times*, January 21, 1960.

47. New York *Times*, February 4, 1960.

48. New York *Times*, February 19, 1960.

49. New York *Times*, February 27, 1975; JTA, *Daily News Bulletin*, February 28, 1975, p. 3.

50. MacDonald, op. cit., p. 121. "According to *The New York Times* Jordan and Iraq 'suspended trade with Cyprus in August 1952.' It is understood that Saudi Arabia also imposed such a prohibition of trade in 1952." Bahti, op. cit., p. 71, n. 13.

51. Bahti, op. cit., p. 5.

52. New York *Times*, February 25, 1960.

53. New York *Times*, April 26, 1959.

54. *Al Ahram*, June 29, 1955.

55. Cairo Radio, June 14, 1955.

56. Radio Ramalla, August 7, 1955.

57. *Al Ahram,* September 2, 1956.

58. *Wall Street Journal,* December 30, 1974.

59. *ADL Bulletin,* May 1966, p. 4.

60. Ibid., pp. 4-5.

61. Ibid., p. 5.

62. New York *Times,* April 13, 1966.

63. *ADL Bulletin,* May 1966, p. 5.

64. New York *Times,* April 14, 1966.

65. Ibid.

66. New York *Times,* April 16, 1966.

67. New York *Times,* May 9, 1966.

68. New York *Times,* November 21, 1966.

69. Ibid.

70. New York *Times,* September 25, 1966.

71. New York *Times,* November 21, 1966.

72. Ibid.

73. New York *Times,* November 27, 1966.

74. New York *Times,* November 25, 1966, and November 26, 1966. Note that Ford sold 20,000 vehicles in the Arab world in 1965, less than 1 percent of its total sales.

75. New York *Times,* November 29, 1966.

76. Ibid.

77. New York *Times,* December 2, 1966.

78. New York *Times,* December 13, 1966.

79. New York *Times,* December 14, 1966.

80. *Wall Street Journal,* March 14, 1975.

81. "List of Boycott Recommendations," *Economic Review of the Arab World,* no. 2 (February 1967): 19.

82. Joint statement of Israel Government Tourist Corporation and American Express Company, June 18, 1958, discussed in Arnold J. Forster to Philip Kentznick (B'nai B'rith), June 18, 1958.

83. *Time,* July 19, 1971.

84. "The Arab Boycott Involves Americans," *Near East Report* (supplement) (May 1965): B-5.

85. *Newsweek,* March 10, 1975; *Time,* March 10, 1975.

86. New York *Times,* February 27, 1975. In August 1975, three major U.S. companies, North American Rockwell, General Telephone and Electronics, and Berkey Photo Corporation, as well as the Rumanian national airline, Tarom, were added to the blacklist for their dealings with Israel. New York *Times,* August 24, 1975.

87. Gervasi, op. cit., p. 134.

88. Remba, op. cit., p. 50.

89. Gervasi, op. cit.

90. Marver Bernstein, *The Politics of Israel* (Princeton, N.J.: Princeton University Press, 1957), p. 187.

91. Remba, op. cit. See also *Time,* July 19, 1971.

92. "The Arab Boycott Involves Americans," *Near East Report,* op. cit., p. B-16.

93. A. Dagan, "The Arab Boycott," in *Israel Yearbook 1966* (Jerusalem: Israel Yearbook Publications, 1966), p. 251. The major problem with this analysis is that the Arabs have had less success in their attempts to influence the economic activities of the giant corporations.

94. Ibid. See also *Chemical Week,* April 6, 1957.

95. New York *Times,* July 7, 1967.

96. *Wall Street Journal,* December 30, 1974.

97. Marwan Iskandar, "Arab Boycott of Israel," *Middle East Forum* 36 (October 1960): 28-30.

98. Dagan, op. cit., p. 252.

99. General Union of the Arab Chambers of Commerce, Industry and Agriculture, *Arab Boycott of Israel: Its Grounds and Its Regulations* (Beirut, 1959), pp. 2, 4.

100. Robert E. Weigand, "The Arab League Boycott of Israel," *Michigan State University Business Topics* (Spring 1968): 70. Note that while Renault is government owned, its officials are free to determine their business policies on a private basis.

101. Ibid. According to the Washington *Post* of October 19, 1959, French-Israeli diplomatic relations were reportedly strained as a result of the Renault case and Israel, shortly thereafter, decided to cancel a contract for a 650-passenger oceanliner that was to have been built in France.

102. It has been argued: "Since both Renault and Air France are owned by the French Government, the[se] two boycott cases were undoubtedly intended as retaliation to French support for Israel during and after the Suez Crisis of 1956." MacDonald, op. cit., p. 120.

103. Memorandum from Forster to ADL regional offices, September 18, 1958, p. 1.

104. Ibid.

105. Ibid., p. 2.

106. Ibid.

107. Ibid.

108. Ibid., p. 3.

109. Ibid.

110. Ibid.

111. Ibid., p. 4.

112. *Wall Street Journal,* March 4, 1975.

113. Susan Dworkin, "The Japanese and the Arab Boycott," *Near East Report* (supplement) (October 1968): 12.

114. Government of Japan, *Japanese Economic Statistics* (Tokyo: Economic Planning Agency, 1966).

115. New York *Times,* August 17, 1969.

116. Dworkin, op. cit., p. 11.

117. Anti-Defamation League, B'nai B'rith, *Japan's Foreign Trade and the Arab Boycott of Israel* (New York: Anti-Defamation League, 1968), p. 8.

118. See, in general, W. S. Hunsberger, *Japan and the United States in World Trade* (New York: Harper and Row, 1964).

119. Ibid.

120. Anti-Defamation League, *Japan's Foreign Trade and the Arab Boycott of Israel,* op. cit., p. 17.

121. *ADL Bulletin,* October 1965, p. 6.

122. *ADL Bulletin,* December 1970, p. 8.

123. In addition, both Tokyo Shibaura Electric Co. and Honda began publicizing copies of invoices in order to prove they had been doing some business with Israel (Dworkin, op. cit., p. 12).

124. New York *Times,* February 26, 1975.

125. *ADL Bulletin,* December 1970, p. 7.

126. Ibid.

127. "Japanese car makers are negotiating with almost all European nations . . ."; quoted in Ibid. It is of interest to note that the Israeli

Government called off a proposed boycott by American customers of Toyota because the Japanese company's agent in the United States was a major contributor to the United Jewish Appeal. Jerusalem *Post Weekly*, June 10, 1975.

128. Ibid.

129. Ibid. In 1969, "press reports from Egypt . . . indicated that the Arab League had lifted a boycott of the Export-Import Bank of Japan in return for a pledge to make no more loans for trade with Israel." New York *Times,* August 17, 1969.

130. New York *Times,* August 6, 1974.

131. Jerusalem *Post Weekly,* March 4, 1975.

132. Dworkin, op. cit., pp. 12-13.

133. Ibid., p. 13.

134. Anti-Defamation League, "Japan Air Lines and the Arab Boycott," mimeographed (New York: Anti-Defamation League, December 1972), pp. 1-4.

135. Memorandum from Phil Baum, director, Commission of International Affairs (CIA), American Jewish Congress, to the Congress' chapter and division Presidents, CIA chapter and division chairmen, regional directors, Regional Council's staff, February 28, 1973.

136. J. K. Banerji, *The Middle East in World Politics* (Calcutta: The World Press Private, 1960), p. 203.

137. New York *Times,* December 22, 1963.

138. Bahti, op. cit., p. 33.

139. Eban, "The Answer to Arab Boycott," op. cit., p. 19.

140. Ibid., p. 21.

141. Banerji, op. cit., p. 338. See also *Time,* July 19, 1971.

142. Pierre Roudot, "Arab Boycott as Myth," *New Outlook* 6, no. 5 (June 1963): 21.

143. Ibid. See also New York *Times,* October 14, 1962.

144. Ernest Teilhac, *Economie Politique Pour Les Arabes* (Paris: R. Pichon et R. Durand-Auzias, 1960), p. 84.

145. *Al Akhbar,* April 5, 1960.

146. *ADL Bulletin,* June 1964, p. 8.

147. New York *Times,* January 28, 1965. It should be noted that the Arab League has taken credit for the collapse of joint ventures in the shipping field among Israel's Zim Line and the governments of Ghana and Sierra Leone. In addition, partial success has been achieved by the Arabs in their anti-Israeli efforts in Somalia and Nigeria. However, Israeli ties with West African countries continue to develop. See MacDonald, op. cit., p. 122.

148. Gervasi, op. cit., p. 133.

149. Weigand, op. cit., p. 75. Hotel companies that establish hotels bearing their names in Israel are not blacklisted if (1) their role in the hotels is limited to technical and administrative supervision; (2) their funds are destined for administrative operations only; (3) the business that they conduct in the Arab states is at least on a par with their activity in Israel; and (4) they do not favor Israel with special publicity. "General Principles for Boycott of Israel," sec. 15.

150. Business International, "Coping with the Arab Boycott of Israel," Management Monograph (New York: Business International, 1964), p. 12.

151. *Near East Report* 9, no. 1 (January 12, 1965): 4.

152. New York *Times,* July 10, 1964.

153. New York *Times,* September 23, 1964.

154. New York *Times,* December 27, 1964.

155. New York *Times,* July 13 and July 14, 1964.

156. New York *Times,* January 5, 1965.

157. Jerusalem *Post,* November 18, 1975.

158. Gervasi, op. cit., p. 133. See also J. C. Hurewitz, *Middle East Politics* (London: Pall Mall Press, 1969), p. 142. According to MacDonald, op. cit., p. 121, "the threat of boycott was also used in 1962-63 against members of the European Economic Community who, the Arabs feared, were about to conclude an agreement [making] . . . Israel an associate member of the European Common Market."

159. Kessler, op. cit.

160. New York *Times,* April 23, 1967. Moreover, it should be noted that, after the June war, Rumania was the sole Soviet bloc country that continued to maintain diplomatic relations with Israel.

161. *Near East Report* 9, no. 24 (November 30, 1965): 95.

162. New York *Times,* November 24, 1968.

163. *Near East Report*, "The Arab Boycott Today" (special survey) (August 1967): B-23.

164. Business International, op. cit., p. 1.

165. Ibid., p. 2.

166. *Middle East Record 1961* (Jerusalem: Reuven Shiloah Research Institute, 1961), p. 204.

167. Bahti, op. cit., pp. 23-24.

168. *Near East Report*, "The Arab Boycott Involves Americans" (supp.) (May 1965): B-5.

169. Malcolm Kerr, *The Arab Cold War: A Study of Ideology in Politics, 1958-67* (London: Oxford University Press, 1967), pp. 53-54. See also Harry B. Ellis, "The Arab-Israeli Conflict Today," in American Assembly, *The United States and the Middle East* (Englewood Cliffs, N.J.: Prentice-Hall, 1964), p. 130.

170. Kerr, op. cit., p. 54.

171. Business International, op. cit., p. 5.

172. New York *Times,* February 27, 1975.

173. New York *Times,* December 17, 1963. In addition, American firms such as Israel Religious Art, Inc., Israel Investors Corporation, Israel Coin Distributors Corporation, Israel Creations, Inc., and Israel American Shipping have received warning letters although the chances are rather remote that these companies hope to engage in business dealings with the Arab countries. See Bahti, op. cit., p. 15.

174. *Near East Report* 9, no. 23 (November 16, 1965): 95.

175. Gervasi, op. cit., p. 132.

176. New York *Times,* April 9, 1966.

177. *Ruz al Yusuf,* April 24, 1961. See *Middle East Record,* op. cit., p. 205.

178. *Near East Report* 9, no. 5 (March 9, 1965): 17.

179. Bahti, op. cit., p. 16.

180. New York *Times,* February 27, 1975.

181. Jerusalem *Post Weekly,* March 4, 1975.

182. *Time,* July 19, 1971.

183. Business International, op. cit., p. 11.

184. Ibid.

185. Ibid., p. 12.

186. Jerusalem *Post Weekly,* March 4, 1975.

187. For a detailed account of the troubles confronting the American President Lines' ship, *President Roosevelt,* in 1965, see *Near East Report* 9, no. 26 (December 28, 1965).

188. New York *Times,* January 10, 1965.

189. Roudot, loc. cit.

190. New York *Times,* March 30, 1975; *Wall Street Journal,* April 4, 1975.

191. Iskandar, op. cit., pp. 28-29. Ellis, in The American Assembly, op. cit., p. 130, claims that Lebanon and Syria derive important income from the increase in Jordanian transit trade caused by Jordan's inability to use the Haifa port: "The opening of Haifa to Jordan might cause the Lebanese port of Beirut to lose more than 20% of its entire transit trade, with the Syrian state railroad suffering even greater loss."

192. Michael Shefer, "The Effect of the Arab-Israeli Rupture on the Economy of the Arab Countries," *New Outlook* 7, no. 9 (November-December 1964): 4-16; Government of Palestine, *Statistics of Imports, Exports and Shipping,* 1938; Government of Palestine, *Statistics of Foreign Trade,* 1944-45.

193. Shefer, op. cit., as cited in Bahti, op. cit., pp. 36-37.

194. Ibid.

195. Ibid., p. 30.

196. Bahti, op. cit., p. 33.

3

World reaction to the Arab Boycott, on the whole, has been unfavorable.[1] We have already seen the negative reaction of the UN Security Council in 1951 and, again, in 1954. Three years later, UN Secretary General Dag Hammarskjold condemned the Boycott as a "deadweight" on the UN efforts for a Middle East settlement.[2]

ISRAEL'S POSITION

Israel's initial reaction to the Boycott was surprising. A feeling persisted, into the early 1970s, that the Boycott would and could cause Israel no harm. Therefore, the strategy was one of complete silence since publicizing Arab actions would increase the importance of these actions in the eyes of the business world.[3] An exception to this silence occurred in 1965 when Israel saw that its silence had been interpreted as an inability to cope with the Arab economic activities.

On February 9, 1965, Israel notified its importers that future dealings with foreign concerns submitting to the Arab Boycott would require a special license and such license would not be forthcoming. The foreign companies immediately affected by the decree were Allgemeine-Telefunken AG, Siemens AG, and Imperial Rundfunk und Fernwerk GMBH of West Germany; Pye, Ltd., of Great Britain; and Hitachi and Matsushita of Japan, all of whom, at that time had succumbed, in one form or another, to Arab pressures.[4] As we have seen, since 1965, both Matsushita and Hitachi have agreed to conduct open business transactions with Israel. However, even as late as 1974, the Israeli government evidenced no desire to compile and publicize the Boycott's activities and effects.

In 1975, however, Israel realized the extent of the economic might wielded by the Arab nations and its error in not preparing a concerted political and economic counterattack against the Boycott's overtures and those who submit to it. Noting how successful, on a limited scale, the ADL's countermeasures have been in the United States, Chaim Herzog, Israel's ambassador-designate to the United Nations, has bemoaned the lack of an organized and coordinated worldwide Jewish reaction to the Boycott:

> Surely this was a subject made-to-measure for the recent World Jewish Congress? This organization could do something effective by channeling its million dollar budgets to coordinating a battle against Arab blackmail. The Zionist Actions Committee and the Board of Governors of the Jewish Agency have met several times in the last eighteen months, but have done nothing to tackle this problem.
>
> Above all, the Government os Israel is to blame because in all the years of the State's existence, there has been insufficient appreciation of the importance of this subject. No instrument has been created capable of reacting in economic warfare and affording leadership and direction to world Jewry in this struggle. This is . . . a subject . . . for a top-level organization in the State and in world Jewry.[5]

Herzog proceeded to call for the convocation of a World Economic Jewish Conference in Jerusalem "to devise an answer to the Arab Boycott and those who submit to it, and mobilize Jewish support for those who oppose Arab blackmail."[6]

In June 1975, Israel announced that Avraham Agmon, former director general of its Finance Ministry, had been appointed to head a new governmental unit on "Matters Concerning Economic Warfare."[7] The anti-Boycott unit, whose plans of action and detailed budget were approved in September 1975, will have a staff both in Israel and the United States and will attempt to coordinate international political, economic, and communal reaction to the Boycott's efforts throughout the world.

The U.S. Reaction

The original U.S. reaction to the Boycott, from the Arab point of view, was highly encouraging. On May 22, 1956, the State Department's Public Service Division issued the following statement:

> [W]e are obliged to recognize that any attempt by this country to force our views on a foreign national would be considered intervention in the domestic affairs of that nation and therefore greatly resented.[8]

In addition, at one time, the State Department felt that the Boycott was merely the work of a few private firms:

> The Department hopes that these instances are in the nature of sporadic, out-of-bounds, actions based on excessive zeal or mis-understanding on the part of certain individuals rather than an indication of fundamental intensification of boycott practice by the Saudi Arabian Government.[9]

These State Department views reflect an attempt to blur an issue that would have damaged the amicable U.S.-Arab relations of the early 1950s.

Yet, as protests by the Jewish community, in general, and Jewish congress-men, in particular, began to publicize the extent and true nature of the Arab undertaking, and as U.S.-Arab relations began to deteriorate for sundry reasons, a shift in policy was seen. As early as July 26, 1956, the U.S. Senate adopted the following resolution (Senate Resolution 323), introduced by Senator Herbert H. Lehman of New York:

> Whereas the protection of the integrity of the United States citizenship and of the proper rights of the United States citizens in the pursuit of lawful trade, travel, and other activities abroad is a principle of the United States sovereignty: and
>
> Whereas it is a primary principle of our nation that there shall be no distinction among United States citizens based on the individual religious affiliations and since any attempt by foreign nations to cre-ate such distinctions among our citizens in the granting of personal or commercial access or any other rights otherwise available to United States citizens generally is inconsistent with our principles: now, therefore, be it
>
> Resolved that it is the sense of the Senate that it regards any such distinction directed against the United States citizens as incom-patible with the relations that should exist among friendly nations, and that in all negotiations between the United States and any for-eign state every reasonable effort should be made to maintain this principle.[10]

In 1960, U.S. concerns received Kuwaiti letters requesting them to "clar-ify" the scope of their relations with Israel and Israeli companies or else be blacklisted in all Arab countries. The State Department protested that this was an unwarranted interference by the Kuwait Boycott Office with the commercial relationships of U.S. firms.[11]

In the same year, Congressmen Wayne Hays and Leonard Farbstein and Senators Paul Douglas and Kenneth Keating introduced amendments to the Mutual Security Act. The Douglas-Hays Amendment expressed the "sense-of-Congress" as being opposed to economic warfare, including boycotts, blockades, and restrictions on the use of international waterways.[12] Following the immediate passage by the House of Representatives of the amendment, Senator William Fulbright unsuccessfully attempted to have it deleted on the Senate floor, alleging that the amendment was the work of "a pressure group in the United States which seeks to inject the Arab-Israeli dispute into domestic politics."[13] In signing the Mutual Security Act, President Eisenhower referred to the amendment as the act's "one regrettable exception." However, as a "sense-of-Congress" provision, the amendment was not of a mandatory nature and the administration announced that it was able to "live with" the law.[14]

Between 1960 and 1965, the Department of State decided to permit the authentication of documents, required by Arab countries, to be furnished for Boycott purpose. This permissive attitude was adopted despite the Arab Boycott requirement that the documents were to be sent to an Arab national Boycott office. However, the State Department "continued to refuse to authenticate documents addressed to the Arab League Central Boycott Office or which contained declarations of creed."[15]

By 1965, demands for stronger, more effective, actions were voiced, especially by congressmen who were beginning to become well informed about the Boycott from constituents' letters. The Johnson administration, however, opposed a strong congressional stand against the Arab Boycott since the U.S. attitude with regard to trade with Communist China, Cuba, North Vietnam, and North Korea was considered to be similar to the Arabs' policy:[16]

> Under-Secretary of State George Ball pointed out that the United States Government, in enforcing these [anti-Communist] programs, sought detailed information from foreign firms and governments concerning their international trade. A law prohibiting American businessmen from furnishing information to Arab authorities might well bring about foreign restrictive legislation that would reduce the availability of information necessary to enforce United States legislation.[17]

The bill that emerged from Congress on June 30, 1965, and that was reluctantly signed by President Johnson on the same day, was an amendment to the Export Control Act, and was enacted and signed largely due to the efforts of Senators Jacob Javits of New York and Harrison Williams of New Jersey.[18] The anti-Boycott amendment required the administration to announce to businessmen, by October 1, 1965, that it was the policy of the United States to oppose practices or boycotts imposed by foreign nations against countries that are friendly to the United States. The government announced that its policy was to "encourage and request" domestic concerns to refuse to take any action or furnish any information that furthers or supports such restrictive trade practices. Recipients of requests for such information were required to notify the Department of Commerce.[19]

The notification was to be on an official Commerce Department form, IA-1014.[20] The form was updated and revised in December 1975 (see Appendix D). Between October 7, 1965, and February 28, 1967, U.S. business firms reported, on Form IA-1014, the receipt of 9,280 requests for information from Arab Boycott offices. These included 4,815 requests for certification that goods were not of Israeli origin; 3,349 demands for certification that the carrying vessels were not blacklisted; 97 requests for certification that the exporter had no subsidiaries or financial interests in Israel; and 559 miscellaneous requests (for example, certification that the insurance company was not blacklisted, or that West German reparations were not involved).[21] There have also been a few hundred requests from Israel directed against the Arab countries' activities.[22]

Arnold Forster, general counsel for the Anti-Defamation League, hailed congressional efforts on behalf of the amendment as "one effective answer to the malevolent interruptions" of American export trade.[23] As was to be expected, Arab reaction to the 1965 amendment to the Export Control Act was vitriolic. While the administration was praised for its opposition to the amendment, the proposal was attacked as a "Zionist maneuver" instigated by "Zionist legislators."[24] However, the intensity of this reaction was mainly due to the Arab countries' erroneous assumption that the law prohibited responses to queries from Boycott offices;[25] when the Arabs were apprised of the actual facts, a general lull in the recriminations ensued.

The Boycott offices were further pacified in October 1966 by the Department of Commerce's announcement that under the amendment the words "requests for information or action" did not apply to (1) shipping or transportation facilities owned, controlled, operated, or chartered by a country or a national of a country friendly to the United States but not friendly to the importing country; or (2) a carrier which stops at a port in a country friendly to the United States but not friendly to the importing country prior to stopping at the port of destination. The rationale behind the department's ruling was that such requests had come from Israeli, Indian, and Pakistani, as well as from Arab, importers and were made only to lessen the risk of the commodity's confiscation and to ensure the safe arrival of the shipment.[26] Many congressmen criticized this ruling.

In addition, the Department of Commerce was criticized

> for publishing business opportunities (including bid invitations) in the *Foreign Commerce Weekly* (now *International Commerce*) when the tender documents contain boycott references. It is argued that even calling attention to these opportunities is a form of recognition and approval of the boycott. Several legislators and groups have urged not only that such opportunities not be published but that our embassies refuse to accept such documents for transmittal to the United States. It should be noted . . . that tender documents containing discriminatory conditions relating to race or religion are not

publicized nor, for that matter, accepted by American embassies. Business opportunities published in *International Commerce* do not indicate the presence or absence of boycott stipulations.[27]

In defense, James H. Bahti contended that the Commerce Department's refusal to publicize the existence of business opportunities in Arab countries "would be a kind of discrimination, in that American firms that wish to trade with Arab countries would be denied a service . . . to which they are entitled."[28]

In September 1975, the ADL filed suit against the Commerce Department and its secretary, Rogers C. B. Morton, on the basis of the department's willingness to issue the business opportunity reports. As a direct result of this litigation and a lawsuit (discussed below) filed by twenty-five congressmen, as well as a shift in the administration's stance vis-a-vis the Boycott, the department, on November 26, 1975, announced that it would no longer issue such reports and would destroy all reports in its possession which referred to tender documents containing Boycott references.[29]

Of parallel interest is an incident, unrelated to the government, which occurred in April 1975. McGraw and Associates, a Florida company with construction interests in the Arab countries, advertised in a Florida newspaper for "immediate job opportunities in [the] Middle East" on a $70 million project. The advertisement warned potential applicants: "We trust that you are aware of the discrimination policies of the Arab world before replying to this ad." Arthur Teitelbaum, the ADL's southern area director, described the advertisement as a "shameful capitulation by an American company to the discriminatory policies of the Arab States." The ADL has filed a complaint against McGraw and Associates with the U.S. Equal Employment Opportunity Commission.[30]

Subsequent to the 1965 amendment, many congressmen expressed a feeling that the nonmandatory features (the words "encourage and request") of the 1965 rules weakened the intent of the legislation and that Form IA-1014 failed to specify penalties for noncompliance with the few mandatory provisions.[31] In 1967, Stanley H. Lowell, cochairman of the congressional Commission on International Affairs, correctly asserted that the 1965 law allowed companies to give Arabs the requested information and at the same time fill out the IA-1014 form.[32]

Through 1974, it was apparent that very few American exporters had been filing the IA-1014 reports. In response to a *Wall Street Journal* request pursuant to the Freedom Information Act, the Commerce Department disclosed that only 785 reports were filed in 1974, down from the range of 4,435 to 7,916 reports filed annually between 1966 and 1971.* During the first three quarters of 1974, those companies that filed reports admitted compliance with the Arab Boycott's conditions in 50 percent to 60 percent of the cases; the remaining companies failed

---

*Due to an aberration, whereby one company filed 21,247 transactions in which it certified it was not using a blacklisted insurance company, the total reached 23,617 in 1972. It dropped to 1,152 in 1973.

to say whether or not they so complied. In the final quarter of 1974, those companies failing to disclose compliance rose to 80 percent of the total reports filed.[33]

In 1975, as a result of the Commerce Department's publicity campaign reminding companies of their obligation to report all requests from Arab countries seeking information relating to the Boycott, reports increased substantially. The total dollar value of transactions described in the reports filed in 1975 exceeded the value of all previous Boycott-related transactions which had been reported since the 1965 passage of the amendment to the Export Administration Act.[34] Concrete information relating to compliance has yet to be disclosed.

In most 1974 cases, the companies' compliance involved certification that goods shipped to an Arab country did not originate from Israel, did not contain Israeli-manufactured material, and were not shipped in a blacklisted vessel or insured by a blacklisted insurance company. Occasionally, companies were requested to certify that they did not have subsidiaries or financial interests in Israel. Since companies were only "encouraged and requested" under the Export Administration Act to refuse to support boycotts, no legal sanctions provided in the act could be imposed upon those companies that complied. Moreover, a confidentiality clause within the act prevented the public from learning the identity of those companies that were approached by the Boycott and that filed the IA-1014 reports. These factors, along with the rise in U.S. exports to Arab nations from $1.74 billion in 1973 and $3.34 billion in 1974 to a value expected to exceed $5 billion in 1975,[35] evidenced a growing need to strengthen American anti-Boycott measures. (For examples of Boycott pressures, see Appendix C.)

On September 26, 1975, the Commerce Department, in response to congressional and organizational pressures, advised Democratic Representative John Moss of California, chairman of the Interstate and Foreign Commerce Subcommittee, that, in the future, every American exporter would be required to state, in Form DIB-621P (the successor to IA-1014), whether it had submitted to and complied with the Arab Boycott.

In November 1975, Secretary of Commerce Morton was cited for contempt by the House Subcommittee on Oversight and Investigations because of his repeated refusal to supply the names of American firms that complied with the Arab Boycott's restrictions.[36] In the same month, twenty-five members of the House of Representatives, led by Congressman Robert F. Drinan of Massachusetts, filed a federal suit accusing Secretary Morton and Interior Secretary Thomas Kleppe of (1) promoting trade between American firms and several Arab nations, of which the latter had blacklisted companies doing business with Israel; and (2) "actively participating in the implementation" of the Boycott by applying its provisions to the selection of American firms bidding to undertake U.S. governmental work in the Middle East.[37]

The congressional suit cited the secretaries for violating the Export Administration Act which proclaims the U.S. opposition to restrictive trade practices of other nations:

The suit accused Kleppe of violating the law by requiring U.S. companies supplying material to the Interior Department's Geological Survey Bureau in the Middle East and North Africa to certify that the steamship and insurance companies they used are not on the Arab's boycott list.

It accused Morton of stating to U.S. exporters that Congress' policy is only a policy and does not legally prohibit them from participating in a boycott.[38]

Shortly thereafter, Morton agreed to provide Congressman Moss's subcommittee with the names of the American firms complying with the Boycott. The agreement, entered into in order to avoid a political confrontation, was conditioned upon a promise from the subcommittee to keep the information confidential.[39] The congressional litigation was dismissed shortly thereafter when Morton and Kleppe agreed to terminate the practices against which the suit had been directed.

Additional pressures in the United States were exerted by certain congressional leaders and Jewish organizations in order to supplement the Export Administration Act with enforcement and penalty clauses and, in addition, to seek new legislation to combat the Arab Boycott. These pressures were the direct result of (1) Senator Frank Church's revelations of the Saudi "Directory of Boycotted Companies and Establishments," which included a list of 1,500 U.S. corporations on the 1970 blacklist; (2) disclosures by the Anti-Defamation League relating to alleged discrimination against Jews by Ashland Chemical Company, Pacific Pump Corporation (a subsidiary of Dresser Industries), Aramco Service Co., Hospital Corporation of America, and International School Services, as well as by two federal agencies, the Army Corps of Engineers and OPIC;[40] and (3) the extensive publicity afforded the agreement by certain banking institutions in London and Paris to exclude Jewish-owned banks from investment syndications.

In testimony before Senator Church's Subcommittee on Multinational Corporations, Colonel William L. Durham, deputy director for military construction for the Army Corps of Engineers, acknowledged that the corps does not assign its Jewish personnel to Saudi Arabia. He claimed, however, that

... the Corps was not aware of the existence of the blacklist, that it had never precluded Jewish-connected U.S. construction contractors or architectural-engineering firms from bidding on projects in Saudi Arabia, and that the Saudi government has never rejected any contractor recommended by the Corps.[41]

Nevertheless, Colonel Durham admitted that it is generally known among contractors that a prerequisite for securing a contract in Saudi Arabia is a work visa and that a company need not apply for a visa, or for selection by the corps, if it has Jewish personnel, and/or employees of Israeli nationality, in key positions within the company.[42]

The corps contended that it was bound by the 1964 agreement between the United States and Saudi Arabia relating to American engineering assistance for military and nonmilitary projects. This agreement provided that Saudi law would govern all arrangements. However, due to the furor relating to the corps' apparent compliance with the Boycott, the agreement has come under scrutiny, especially given Colonel Durham's admission that all contracts undertaken by the corps were approved by the State Department.[43] In December 1975, the American Jewish Congress filed suit in federal district court against Secretary of State Henry Kissinger, Secretary of the Treasury William E. Simon, Secretary of Commerce Elliot Richardson, and Secretary of the Interior Kleppe. The suit charged the federal government was a "silent partner" in Saudi Arabia's "religious bigotry against Jews" and sought an injunction barring the secretaries from implementing a 1974 U.S.-Saudi agreement calling for cooperation between the two countries in the fields of economics, technology, and industry.[44]

While the State Department urged that quiet diplomacy, rather than confrontation, was needed in the Saudi situation, President Ford, at a press conference held in Florida on February 26, 1975, denounced Arab attempts to discriminate against financial institutions or individuals on religious or ethnic grounds:

> Such discrimination is totally contrary to the American tradition and repugnant to American principles ... and has no place in the free practice of commerce as it has flourished in this country. . . . [A]ny allegation of discrimination will be fully investigated and appropriate action taken under the laws of the United States.[45]

President Ford immediately implemented his antidiscrimination stance by ordering (1) the Commerce Department to investigate the Arab Boycott's impact on businesses in the United States; (2) the State and Justice Departments to review the possibility of controlling the Boycott through international law; (3) the Defense Department to investigate the Boycott's role within the military services; and (4) the Justice Department to ascertain whether or not the Boycott's actions violated the civil rights and/or antitrust laws.[46]

Responding favorably to President Ford's statement, Rabbi Arthur Hertzberg, president of the American Jewish Congress, joined with 130 members of the House of Representatives in calling upon Attorney General Edward S. Levi not to wait for individual complaints but to exercise the power vested in him pursuant to Section 707(a) of Title VII of the 1964 Civil Rights Act. This section authorizes the attorney general to bring legal action against employers who practice job discrimination when he has "reasonable cause" to believe that such discrimination exists.[47]

An investigation somewhat similar in scope already had been commenced by New York State's Attorney General Louis J. Lefkowitz. Lefkowitz learned that the Kuwait International Investment Company (KIIC) had withdrawn as comanager of a $50 million loan to the Mexican government, and a $25 million bond issue by Volvo, the Swedish automobile maker. The reason given for KIIC's withdrawal was that the investment banking firm of Lazard Freres & Co., a blacklisted company, was among the underwriters that had been invited by Merrill, Lynch, Pierce, Fenner & Smith, Inc., to participate in placing the securities with their customers.[48]

Lefkowitz charged that possible violations of the state's antitrust, civil rights, and securities laws had occurred: "This is the first instance that I know of where our free market in securities has come under possible pressure and coercive tactics based on bigotry and demeanor unbecoming the securities market."[49] In furtherance of his investigation, Lefkowitz sent a questionnaire to brokers, dealers, and underwriters asking them to disclose attempts at anti-Jewish intimidation or coercion.

In an exhibition of strength worthy of a corporate giant, Merrill Lynch announced that it would proceed with its two international offerings without KIIC's association.[50] This action evoked the immediate praise of Senators Javits and Williams who, at the same time, in a letter to Treasury Secretary Simon, asked Simon to "promulgate, where possible, such regulations as may be necessary to prevent the occurrence of any such religious discrimination [and] ... to propose new legislation if needed to prevent such discrimination."[51]

On January 27, 1975, and again in early March 1975, Senator Williams offered legislation that would prohibit foreign individuals, companies, or governments which participate in economic boycotts, from investing in the United States. The Williams Amendment to the Securities and Exchange Act of 1934, cosponsored by Senator Javits, would bar an investment of a foreign individual, seeking to acquire 5 percent or more of a domestic corporation's stock, if the investor had forced or attempted to force other firms to boycott an American business firm because of its dealings with a foreign country with which the United States has diplomatic relations. In addition, the president of the United States would be empowered to veto the purchase if, in his view, it would injure the U.S. domestic interest or national security. Furthermore, a foreign investor who is shown to have been guilty of such practices in the past may be divested of his interest.[52]

The Ford administration opposed Williams's proposed legislation on the premise that existing laws were adequate to control the Boycott. Testifying before the Subcommittee on Securities of the Senate Banking, Housing and Urban Affairs Committee, Jack F. Bennett, undersecretary of the treasury for monetary affairs, contended that foreign investment is contributing to the dynamism of the American economy. He said: "Let us not make the surveillance so oppressive as to drive it [foreign investment] away. We need it." Senator Williams, however, noted that Bennett formerly was an executive of Exxon.[53] In an effort to evidence a sense of concern, Bennett announced that an interagency committee would be established by President Ford to issue periodic reports to the president's Economic Policy Board. This committee would attempt to ensure that foreign investment in the United States was consistent with the national interest.[54]

President Ford, shortly thereafter, buttressed the administration's position that the executive branch was equipped to fight the Boycott without congressional assistance. On November 20, 1975, the president sent to the cabinet detailed instructions regarding new measures by the U.S. government to assure that its antidiscriminatory policies would be effectively and fully implemented.[55]

In response to presidential prodding as well as to the aforementioned ADL suit, Secretary Morton issued a written statement which declared:

> The United States Department of Commerce will not disseminate or make available for inspection any information on trade opportunities obtained from documents or other materials which are known to contain boycott conditions that seek to impose or foster a restrictive trade practice or boycott against another country friendly to the United States.[56]

At the same time, a letter dispatched by the Federal Reserve Board to U.S. banks stated:

> The participation of a U.S. bank, even passively, in efforts by foreign nationals to effect boycotts against foreign countries friendly to the United States—particularly where such boycott efforts may cause discrimination against United States citizens or business—is in the Board's view, a misuse of the privileges and benefits conferred upon Banking institutions.[57]

Moreover, new State Department regulations prohibited the department from giving certification "to a document when it has good reason to believe that the certification is required for an unlawful or improper purpose." Documents containing clauses which are intended to assist boycotts "shall be considered contrary to public policy for the purpose of these regulations."[58] An additional regulation, directed toward the Saudi Arabian government's refusal to issue visas for American Jewish servicemen or government employees to enter the country, barred U.S. government officials from assigning personnel overseas on the basis of discriminatory foreign rules.[59]

Notwithstanding the president's view of the executive's role in the Arab Boycott conflict, the Congress and the national Jewish organizations must be regarded as important additional sources of leadership as well as new ideas and approaches with regard to resisting the Boycott. In fact, were it not for congressional and organizational pressures, it is doubtful that the Ford administration would have assumed and adopted its anti-Boycott stance.

In early March 1975, Senator Williams and Senator Richard S. Schweiker of Pennsylvania introduced a resolution, and Senator Adlai Stevenson III introduced legislation, calling for measures to combat blacklisting practices in international trade. The measures included, inter alia, (1) presidential authority to curtail American corporations' investments in, or transactions with, countries that engage in boycotts or restrictive trade practices; (2) a requirement that the Arab Boycott's overtures, and any intended compliance with the same, be made public; and (3) presidential justification for continuing foreign aid or military sales to countries practicing discrimination.[60]

At the same time, Senator Edward M. Kennedy asked the government to investigate its guarantees of private investments in Saudi Arabia in view of the Arab blacklist policy. Kennedy charged that, as a result of the abovementioned 1974 agreement between OPIC and the Saudis, the U.S. government was "implicitly acquiescing, approving and participating in" the Arab policy of discrimination.[61]

In late March 1975, Representative Elizabeth Holtzman proposed legislation that would impose severe criminal fines or imprisonment, as well as civil treble damages, upon any company, or corporate executive, involved in a boycott against businesses which employ Jews or persons of Israeli national origin, or do business with Israel. Similar penalties and damages would be imposed upon those business entities succumbing to the Boycott's coercion. Congressman Peter Rodino, cosponsor of the measure, and chairman of the House Judiciary Committee, announced that he would conduct hearings before the committee regarding the legislation.[62]

At the same time, Congressman Drinan, on April 14, 1975, introduced legislation which would prohibit the furnishing of information by a corporation with regard to its employees, stockholders, and officers and the companies and nations with which it deals or in which it maintains investments.[63] Furthermore, the Drinan bill would prohibit the refusal to deal or to do business with any nation, corporation, or person because of pressure from a "foreign agent" (the latter is given a broad definition). Although these prohibitions are now included in Commerce Department regulations appearing in Form DIP-621P, the Drinan bill, in addition, would provide for the revocation of export licenses and/or privileges of any exporter complying with the Boycott, require the secretary of commerce to report his findings in this regard to the Equal Employment Opportunity Commission, and allow the secretary to issue such further regulations as he deemed necessary. Moreover, the bill offered corporations and individuals a civil remedy to secure injunctive relief. At the same time, Senator William Roth, a member of the Senate Finance Committee, announced his plan to introduce legislation prohibiting any new investments in the United States by governments practicing discrimination.[64]

In 1975, too, the American Jewish Congress (AJC), in conjunction with the Anti-Defamation League and the American Jewish Committee, proposed

legislation which would consolidate and buttress many of the highlights of the
Drinan and Holtzman bills. This legislation included (1) the imposition of criminal penalties of five years' imprisonment, $100,000 fines, or both upon those
who discriminate on behalf of, or in compliance with, the Arab Boycott; and
(2) the award to Boycott victims of civil remedies, including injunctive relief, a
mandatory minimum recovery in damages of $5,000, as well as punitive and
treble damages and reasonable attorneys' fees. Moreover, a criminal conviction
under the AJC's bill would constitute a per se violation of the civil proscriptions
of the statute. It was the AJC's hope to incorporate certain of its proposals
within one or both of the Drinan-Holtzman bills.[65]

Concurrently, the AJC prepared a memorandum, directed to President
Ford, enumerating the legal recourse presently available to counter the Boycott's activities in the United States. The memorandum, inter alia, urged the
president (1) to direct the secretary of the treasury to issue Boycott-related
regulations under Title 15 of the U.S. Code, Section 73 (the Federal Trade
Commission Act), which imposes a double import duty upon any article imported into the United States under any unlawfully restrictive agreement;
(2) pursuant to Section 77 of Title 15 of the U.S. Code, to deny shipping and
clearance privileges to vessels, and to detain such vessels of any country, engaged
in the current war against Israel, that withholds facilities of commerce to American ships or citizens; (3) to instruct the U.S. Maritime Commission to amend its
regulations under Title 64 of the U.S. Code, Section 815 (the Shipping Act), in
order to prohibit Arab buyers from requiring American sellers to ship their
goods only on vessels that are not on the blacklist; (4) to order the comptroller
of the currency to obtain cease and desist orders against banks that, in violation
of Title 12 of the U.S. Code, Section 1818(b) (the Federal Deposit Insurance
Act), verify letters of credit containing provisions enforcing Boycott policies,
or that follow Boycott directives for the purpose of obtaining Arab deposits or
investments; and (5) to request the Federal Trade Commission (FTC) to utilize
the "unfair or deceptive acts or practices" provisions of the FTC Act against the
Arab Boycott.[66]

One maritime incident that occurred in the United States indicated that,
without strong legislation, open opposition to the Boycott may not be fully
effective. On April 13, 1960, American seamen and longshoremen picketed the
Egyptian ship *Cleopatra* on her arrival in New York, to protest the United Arab
Republic's blacklisting of ships trading with Israel or calling on Israeli ports.
They claimed that such blacklisting had threatened job opportunities for U.S.
seamen.[67] Suits by the ship's owner, the Khedival Mail Line of Alexandria, to
restrain the picketing proved unsuccessful[68] and, to add to Arab discomfort,
the U.S. Senate, by a 45-39 vote, adopted a foreign aid bill with a section
giving the president discretionary authority to withhold assistance from nations
obstructing the free navigation of international waterways.[69] Only after the
Arab countries' stevedores and dock workers began picketing U.S. ships,[70] and

after George Meany, president of the AFL-CIO, was convinced by U.S. officials to intervene, was the picketing stopped. The unions threatened to resume picketing if the Department of State reneged on its pledge to investigate the union's complaints and to intensify diplomatic efforts to protect U.S. ships and seamen from Arab discrimination.[71] However, no further action was taken by the State Department with regard to this matter.

The publicity, and resulting legislative proposals, engendered by post-1973 Boycott activities clearly disturbed the Arab countries. Publicly, Boycott spokesmen insisted that "the Boycott has grown new teeth, and the din in the West is evidence that they can bite."[72] Privately, however, during a 1975 meeting in Cairo, the Boycott Committee took steps to ease the situation by postponing, for six months, action on a proposal by "hard-liners" calling for tighter restrictions on certain blacklisted banks.[73]

In addition, Mohammed Mahgoub, head of the Boycott Office, reiterated that there was no Arab discrimination against Jews and that a number of Jewish businesses were doing well in the Arab countries. He claimed that the Boycott was a "legitimate means of self-defense."[74] Similarly, Khalid Abu Saud, the director of the Investment Department of Kuwait's Finance Ministry, declared that the Boycott was "only a matter of self-preservation" and condemned the Western protests against the blacklist as "anti-Arab xenophobia."[75]

GOVERNMENTAL REACTION OUTSIDE THE UNITED STATES

The official Canadian response to the Boycott has been one of caution. In 1964, the minister of trade declared that a firm's reaction to Arab threats should be determined solely by the firm's policies and interests. Furthermore: "Upon [a firm's] request for assistance, the Canadian government is prepared to consider what actions might be useful and appropriate under the circumstances."[76]

In general, other Western countries' reactions, especially prior to the 1973 Yom Kippur war, have been unfavorable and recriminatory. Chambers of commerce in Italy and Scandinavia have told exporters that they no longer will be given negative certificates of origin,[77] and the International Chamber of Commerce has issued a similar ruling.[78] In October 1964, Harold Wilson stated that his Labour party condemned the Arab Boycott and expressed the hope that the entire commercial community would resist these pressures.[79]

Much earlier, in 1956, the Central Organization for Foreign Economic Relations at The Hague advised members of the Dutch branch of the International Chamber of Commerce not to supply Arab importers with information about the number of Jews working in Dutch export houses.[80] In addition, on September 23, 1957, William Drees, foreign minister of the Netherlands, reiterated that his government would resist all Arab Boycott measures infringing upon Dutch interests. He declared that, as a member of the United Nations, Holland "shares responsibility" for Israel's existence and that the Boycott is "illegal and conflicts with the Armistice agreements."[81] Belgium's response was similar:

> On June 8, 1964, Paul Henri-Spaak, Belgium's Foreign Minister, said in the Belgian Senate that he had called in an Iraqi diplomat to express Belgium's displeasure over Arab threats against Belgian firms planning to participate in the International Fair at Tel Aviv. The Foreign Minister added that Belgium's Minister for External Trade, Henry Brasseur, would be present at "Belgium Day" at the Tel Aviv Fair on June 18, and that he himself would visit Israel from June 17 to June 21, 1964.[82]

The Australian government, in 1964, presented its view of the Boycott in the following response to questions stemming from Qantas Airways' decision to abandon plans to open an office in Tel Aviv: (1) The Arab League is not an official organization and has no international standing;[83] (2) Australia's policy is one of friendly relations with both the Arab countries and Israel; and (3) the Australian government "would ... carefully consider any attempts made to interfere with the freedom of Australian businessmen to trade freely in any part of the world."[84] In addition, the minister for trade and industry noted that Australia bought about A$45 million worth of goods from Arab countries and sold to the Arabs only A$10 million worth of goods annually.[85] In April of the following year, the minister stated that if an Australian firm were to complain about any interruption in trade due to the Boycott, the government would consider, at that time, what it might do, if anything.[86]

Subsequent to October 1973, the major volte-face has occured in Great Britain where, due to the country's dire economic straits, the Labour government has displayed a willingness to cater to Arab interests and pressures. In early February 1975, "reliable sources" disclosed that a number of major European banking houses connected with prominent Jewish families, including N. M. Rothschild & Sons, S. G. Warburg & Co., and Lazard Freres, were being excluded from syndicates, or fund-raising groups, regarding a series of routine international financings because of pressure from Kuwaiti and Arab banks dominated by Kuwaiti interests.[87] In many cases, the excluded banking houses would have been among the leaders in raising the desired funds because of their traditional banking relationships. However, these institutions suddenly found themselves barred from the syndications.

In response to this Arab threat, Gerald Thompson, chairman of the board of the large investment bank, Kleinwort, Benson, Ltd., contended that the London financial community was in no position to oppose the Boycott.[88] Thompson stated: "Our business is to raise money for our customers."[89] He admitted that, when first asked to arrange for a $25 million loan for Marubeni Corporation, the Japanese trading company, Marubeni had specifically asked Kleinwort, Benson to "look for money in the Middle East."[90] Thompson concluded that his banking house, which has effected, and continues to effect, extensive financings in the United States as well as in Western Europe, would continue to respond to Arab requests to prevent Jewish banks from taking part in loan syndications with Arab participants.[91]

Following Thompson's public statement, S. G. Warburg & Co. discreetly protested to the British government this flagrant acquiescence to the pressures of the Arab Boycott. However, the government shocked Warburg and others, in England and throughout the world, by expressing concern not for the blacklisted companies but, rather, for the exigencies of the moment, namely the British need for Arab economic assistance. In a statement attempting to represent Great Britain's credo as well as its apologia, Chancellor of the Exchequer Denis Healey explained:

> Somehow or other, we must find means of helping the oil producers, to channel their surplus funds into productive investment from which we can all benefit ... [Neither Britain nor the other oil-consuming nations should] ... impose our blueprints ... [on how the Arabs dispose of their new oil wealth in the West].[92]

In response to a parliamentary question relating to what the government was doing about the Boycott, Britain's undersecretary of state for trade, Eric Deakins, stated:

> Her Majesty's Government deplores all trade boycotts other than those internationally supported and sanctioned by the UN and, while the position is explained to interested traders, any subsequent decision is a matter for the commercial judgment of the firm concerned.[93]

Similarly, the British foreign trade minister, Peter Shore, has merely "advised" those companies approached by the Boycott to stand firm.[94]

Given the British government's stance, it is not surprising that some companies have already proceeded to cut their ties with Israel. British Leyland is the best example. For years, it operated a truck plant in Israel which produced many of the trucks which now haul merchandise over Israel's roads and munitions for its army. In 1972, however, after incurring serious financial losses, Lord Stokes, chairman of the board of Leyland, signed an agreement to help Egypt build a new $115 million Landrover assembly plant.[95] The quid pro quo sub silentio was Leyland's announcement that its factory in Israel would be closed. Moreover, the company ceased to supply Israel with imported vehicles and spare parts, although Egypt allowed Leyland to fulfill its existing contracts with Israel in order to prevent extensive, and well-publicized, litigation in the courts.[96]

A sense of deja vu overcomes the observer of Leyland's flirtation with the Arab Boycott. Like Renault in 1959, Leyland has sought to cater to the burgeoning economic market in the Arab countries. However, although as of 1976 four years have passed since Leyland signed its agreement with Egypt, construction work on the Landrover assembly plant has not begun and the Egyptians reportedly have become more interested in the American-built Jeeps.[97]

As Felix Kessler of *The New Republic* noted, the controversy in Great Britain with regard to the Arab Boycott has been muted to an extent unimaginable in the United States. Not one editorial has appeared in the *Times* of London with regard to the Boycott. However, given the small Jewish population in Great Britain, 450,000 out of a total of 55 million, British Jewry has maintained a low profile, preferring to counterattack the Boycott by "working quietly and reasonably with reasonable people."[98]

However, extensive publicity and public pressure against the Boycott's activities are the strongest defenses to the inroads achieved by the Boycott. This fact belatedly was recognized by Justin Kornberg who, in 1975, organized an Anti-Boycott Committee in Britain.[99] Even a minority, comprising less than 1 percent of a country's population, given the righteousness of its cause, can turn an apparent communal defeat into a rout for the Arab Boycott. Without publicity and protest, however, the fate of British Jewry, and Jewish banking companies within Great Britain, is foreordained.

In France, French bankers and officials were embarrassed by the disclosure that Lazard Freres & Cie. of Paris, which is Catholic-owned but has close ties to Jewish-owned Lazard Freres in New York, had been excluded from two $25 million financings involving state-owned companies, Air France and Compaigne du Rhone. This exclusion had been as a result of pressure from Kuwaiti and Libyan investment establishments.[100]

Immediately thereafter, in early February 1975, Jean Guyot, the president of Lazard Freres, called on Finance Minister Jean-Pierre Fourcade to present a formal complaint. The French newspapers printed many articles on the general subject of the Boycott and its syndication activities. As a result of the adverse publicity and, to some extent, a realization that Arab economic incursions were becoming overbearing, the Banque Nationale De Paris, on February 11, 1975, decided to postpone indefinitely a planned $40 million to $60 million Eurodollar issue for Electricite de France. Both the bank and the electric company are nationalized.[101]

Shortly thereafter, the French state-owned railway system revealed that it was using three blacklisted institutions, Banque Rothschild and Lazard Freres, both of Paris, and S. G. Warburg & Co. of London, to assist in a $40 million loan. Leading the syndicate was Banque de Paris et des Pays-Bas, one of the largest, privately-owned, banks in France. The syndicate also included the three large, state-owned institutions—Banque Nationale de Paris, Credit Lyonnais, and Societe Generale—as well as two other large European banks, Banque de Bruxelles, S. A., and the Swiss Bank Corporation.[102]

Moreover, on March 29, 1975, as described earlier, several French bankers announced that they had developed a plan to circumvent the Boycott and allow

Jewish participation in the syndications. Clearly, this plan was devised with the imprimatur of the French government and reflected the government's search for "a sophisticated way of handling an unfortunate situation that no one wants to see made worse."[103]

The Arab Boycott offices, along with the Kuwaiti, Lebanese, and Libyan investment banks, have attempted to apply similar pressures to West German financial institutions. The West Germans, in general, are reported to have repulsed this Arab coercion,[104] although several West German companies, under pressure from the Boycott, abruptly discontinued trade relations with Israel, and certain German chambers of commerce indirectly have supported the Boycott by issuing certifications that particular firms do not trade with Israel.[105]

Turning to the Common Market countries en bloc, the Treaty of Rome, the "constitution" of the European Economic Community (EEC), bans "unfair competition," and all Common Market agreements with Arab countries contain a nondiscrimination clause. Unfair competition may arise when a company refuses to deal with Israel in order to secure Arab contracts while its competitor rejects all Boycott demands and, as a result, is barred from future economic ties with the Arabs. In the view of Dan Halperin of the anti-Boycott division of Israel's Finance Ministry, any "rider," written or tacit, appended to an agreement between an Arab country or company and a Common Market company, which nullifies the Common Market nondiscrimination clause, is a violation of the Treaty of Rome.[106] Algeria, in order to conclude an agreement whereby it would receive $137 million in EEC loans and grants, has been forced to agree to the inclusion of the nondiscrimination clause.[107]

In the Far East, Japan continues to display a pro-Arab policy, reflecting the anxiety of the government of Premier Takeo Miki over oil prices and supplies. In January 1975, Japanese officials announced that Japan would side with the Arabs in the event of any renewed hostilities in the Middle East, from which region Japan receives approximately 85 percent of her oil. Furthermore, "greater economic cooperation" with the Arab nations would commence[108] and, to this end, on March 2, 1975, Saudi Arabia and Japan signed an economic and technical cooperation agreement. The agreement called for the dispatch of Japanese technicians to Saudi Arabia, a joint economic committee, and Japanese investments in Saudi Arabia.[109] Whether or not it is mere coincidence that Sony Corporation, soon thereafter, was removed from the Boycott blacklist will be discovered through the measured scrutiny to be applied by the Anti-Defamation League to Sony's future dealings with Israel.

NOTES

1. "Firms in at least 60 countries have been boycotted. Of these countries, 13 are African, 11 Asian and 11 Latin American. Yet, firms in only one Communist country—Yugoslavia—have been [boycotted], . . . though ships of at least 6 Communist countries

[Bulgaria, Communist China, East Germany, Poland, Rumania, and Yugoslavia] have been blacklisted." James H. Bahti, *The Arab Economic Boycott of Israel* (Washington, D.C.: The Brookings Institution, 1967), pp. 58, 78 (n. 1).

  2. New York *Times*, August 9, 1957.

  3. A. Dagan, "The Arab Boycott," in *Israel Yearbook 1966* (Jerusalem: Israel Yearbook Publications, 1966).

  4. New York *Times,* February 10, 1965.

  5. Jerusalem *Post Weekly,* March 25, 1975.

  6. Ibid.

  7. Jerusalem *Post Weekly,* June 3 and 10, 1975.

  8. Presidents of major American Jewish organizations, *A Report on the Arab Boycott Against Americans,* mimeographed (New York: 1958), p. 21.

  9. Assistant Secretary of State Morton to Senator Lehman, December 15, 1953.

  10. *Facts* 16, no. 1 (January 1965): 298.

  11. New York *Times,* August 28, 1960.

  12. U.S. Congress, House, 86th Congress, 2nd Sess., Mutual Security Act and Related Agencies Appropriation Bill, Sec. 2(f), 1960.

  13. U.S. Congress, Senate, 86th Congress, 2nd Sess., *Congressional Record,* April 29, 1960, p. 8976.

  14. Bahti, op. cit., p. 41.

  15. Ibid., p. 55.

  16. *Near East Report* 9, no. 10 (May 18, 1965): 37.

  17. Bahti, op. cit., p. 43.

  18. New York *Times,* July 1, 1965.

  19. *Near East Report* 9, no. 19 (September 21, 1965): 73.

  20. *Near East Report* 9, no. 23 (November 16, 1965): 91.

  21. *Near East Report*, "The Arab Boycott Today" (special survey) (August 1967): B-27.

  22. New York *Times*, February 27, 1966.

  23. *ADL Bulletin* (February 1965): 6.

  24. For example, *al Gumhuriya* (Cairo), May 8, 1965.

  25. Bahti, op. cit., p. 46.

  26. Ibid., p. 48.

  27. Ibid., p. 52.

  28. Ibid., p. 53.

  29. Jerusalem *Post,* November 18 and 28, 1975.

  30. *Jewish Advocate,* May 1, 1975.

  31. *Near East Report,* "The Arab Boycott Today," op. cit., p. B-23.

  32. New York *Times,* March 27, 1967.

  33. *Wall Street Journal,* March 14, 1975.

  34. New York *Times,* July 19, 1975.

  35. Ibid. U.S. Under-Secretary of Commerce, James A. Baker, has predicted that U.S. exports to the Arab countries are expected to reach $10 billion by 1980, and each billion of that total "represents 40,000 to 70,000 jobs for American workers," Sol Stern, "Abetting the Arab Boycott," Jerusalem *Post* 12, no. 6 (March 23, 1976).

  36. Jerusalem *Post*, November 18, 1975.

  37. Ibid.

  38. Ibid.

  39. Jerusalem *Post,* November 27 and December 11, 1975.

  40. Subsequently, OPIC apologized for the incident and Ashland Chemical and Pacific Pump announced that they were prepared to do business with Israel. Arnold Forster,

"The Arab Boycott: An Interim Report." *ADL Bulletin* (June 1975): 2. The ADL has filed legal charges with the Equal Employment Opportunity Commission (EEOC) against Bendix, Aramco Service, Hospital Corporation of America, and International School Services. *Jewish Advocate,* June 12, 1975.

41. *Business Week,* March 17, 1975.

42. Ibid.

43. Ibid.

44. Jerusalem *Post,* December 18, 1975. The AJC suit is a class action brought by the AJC, four of its officials, and two private citizens who were denied admission into Saudi Arabia because they are Jews.

45. New York *Times,* February 27, 1975.

46. *Business Week,* March 17, 1975.

47. *Daily News Bulletin* (Jewish Telegraph Agency), February 27, 1975, p. 2, and *Near East Report* (March 12, 1975): 3.

48. New York *Times,* February 13, 1975.

49. New York *Times,* March 5, 1975.

50. New York *Times,* February 13, 1975.

51. New York *Times,* February 15, 1975.

52. *Near East Report* (March 12, 1975): 46.

53. *Daily News Bulletin,* March 5, 1975, p. 1.

54. Ibid.

55. U.S., White House, *Statement by the President*, November 20, 1975.

56. U.S. Secretary of Commerce Rogers Morton, *Circular Letter* (Washington, D.C.: Government Printing Office, November 26, 1975).

57. Federal Reserve Board, *Circular Letter* (Washington, D.C.: Government Printing Office, December 12, 1975). It should be noted, however, that the Federal Reserve Board chairman was forced by pressures exerted by several major banks to issue a clarifying letter in January 1976, wherein he stated that the earlier circular "was not intended to create new legal obligations for banks." He further tended to vitiate the earlier circular by stating that the primary responsibility for implementing and enforcing U.S. policy on the Boycott rested with the U.S. Department of Commerce, which has previously been shown to vacillate in its policies toward the Boycott. Sol Stern, "How to Lift the Boycott," Jerusalem *Post* 10, no. 3 (March 26, 1976).

58. U.S. Department of State, Regulation 131.2 ("Refusal of Certification for Unlawful Purpose").

59. Jerusalem *Post*, November 23, 1975.

60. *Near East Report* (March 12, 1975): 47. The cosponsors of the Williams-Schweiker resolution included Senators Allen, Bayh, Beall, Bentsen, Biden, Case, Church, Clark, Cranston, Domenick, Fong, Garn, Gravel, Hart, Hartke, Humphrey, Javits, Leahy, Mathias, McGee, McGovern, Mondale, Moss, Muskie, Nelson, Packwood, Proxmire, Ribicoff, Roth, Scott, Stafford, Stone, Symington, Tunney, and Weicker.

61. *Near East Report* (March 26, 1975): 56.

62. Ibid.

63. U.S. Congressman Robert Drinan, "A Bill to Prohibit Actions by United States Exporters which have the Purpose and/or Effect of Supporting Restrictive Trade Practice or Boycott Imposed Against Countries Friendly to the United States by other Foreign Countries," H.R. 5913, April 14, 1975, 94th Cong., 1st sess.

64. Marie Syrkin, "The Elders of Araby," *Midstream,* April 1975, p. 4.

65. On January 20, 1976, President Ford supported the AJC's position regarding civil remedies when he urged Congress to pass legislation to allow Boycott or blacklist victims to sue for damages. Jerusalem *Post,* January 21, 1976.

66. American Jewish Congress, *American Law vs. The Arab Boycott* (A Memorandum to the President of the United States), April 1975, pp. 1-2.

67. New York *Times,* April 14, 1960.

68. New York *Times,* April 16, April 24, April 26, and May 5, 1960.

69. New York *Times,* May 3, 1960.

70. New York *Times,* May 1 and May 3, 1960.

71. New York *Times,* May 7, 1960.

72. New York *Times,* March 4, 1975.

73. *Newsweek,* March 10, 1975.

74. New York *Times,* February 28, 1975.

75. New York *Times,* March 4, 1975.

76. Bahti, op. cit., p. 59, citing *Hansard,* February 19, 1964, p. 9.

77. New York *Times,* April 16, 1966.

78. Abba Eban, "The Answer to Arab Boycott," *The Israel Yearbook 1966* (Jerusalem: Israel Yearbook Publications, 1966), p. 21.

79. Ibid., p. 20.

80. *Netherland News Bulletin,* September 21, 1957. See also *Facts* (Anti-Defamation League), 12, no. 2, (March-April 1957): 101.

81. Presidents of major American Jewish Organizations, op. cit., p. 23.

82. *Facts* 12, no. 1 (January 1965): 298.

83. Bahti rejects this contention, stating, "The League has a permanent observer at the United Nations," in op. cit., p. 78, n. 6.

84. Government of Australia, *Parliamentary Debates,* September 15, 1964, as cited in Bahti, op. cit., p. 60.

85. Ibid.

86. Government of Australia, *Parliamentary Debates,* April 29, 1965, as cited in Bahti, op. cit., p. 60.

87. New York *Times,* February 8, 1975.

88. New York *Times,* February 11, 1975.

89. New York *Times,* February 12, 1975.

90. Ibid.

91. Ibid.

92. Felix Kessler, "Knuckling Under," *The New Republic,* March 8, 1975. In February 1976, British firms that wanted to trade with Arab states were being given 90 days "to get rid of their Jewish directors," Jerusalem *Post* 7, no. 7 (February 24, 1976).

93. Ibid.

94. Jerusalem *Post,* January 4, 1976.

95. *Wall Street Journal,* December 30, 1974; and *Newsweek,* February 24, 1975.

96. *Britain and Israel,* no. 41 (February 1975): 3. Another British company that plans to abandon its long involvement in Israeli industry is Unilever, whose wholly-owned subsidiary, Blue Band, is Israel's main producer of margarine. In May 1974, Unilever suddenly announced its intention to sell its entire interest in this profitable venture, thereby raising a strong inference that it was yielding to the Arab Boycott. Jerusalem *Post Weekly,* May 20, 1975.

97. Jerusalem *Post,* January 8, 1975.

98. Ibid.

99. Jerusalem *Post,* January 4, 1976.

100. New York *Times,* February 22, 1975; and *Newsweek,* February 24, 1975.

101. New York *Times,* February 12, 1975.

102. New York *Times,* February 22, 1975.

103. New York *Times,* March 30, 1975.

104. New York *Times,* February 8, 1975.
105. Jerusalem *Post,* December 19, 1975.
106. Jerusalem *Post,* January 4, 1976.
107. Jerusalem *Post,* January 19, 1976.
108. New York *Times,* January 25, 1975.
109. New York *Times,* March 3, 1975.

4

LAW AND THE BOYCOTT

PRESENT STATUS OF THE LAW

Several legal weapons exist in the United States with which the government, corporations, and individuals may combat Arab Boycott activity.

Foremost among these weapons is Section 1 of the Sherman Antitrust Act which enjoins any agreement, combination, or conspiracy in restraint of inter-state, or international, trade. Thus, the attorney general may bring an antitrust suit against an American company that conspires with an Arab government, or a foreign financial institution, to preclude a Jewish firm from a particular loan syndication or other contractual relationship. Similarly, (1) an individual who is discharged by a company due to Arab protestations relating to his Jewish or Israeli origin, (2) a corporation wronged by the Boycott or those complying with its dictates, and/or (3) the attorney general, may sue under the Sherman Act.

On January 17, 1976, the Justice Department filed an antitrust suit in the U.S. District Court in San Francisco against the Bechtel Corporation. The suit charged Bechtel with (1) refusing the deal with blacklisted U.S. subcontractors on major projects in Arab countries and (2) requiring subcontractors with which Bechtel dealt to follow the same policy when they served as general contractors in such countries.[1] Such antitrust actions, if brought by an individual or a corporation, may result in the award of treble damages to a successful plaintiff, and these damages, prior to being trebled, may include lost earning power and actual, foreseeable, and consequential damages.

In addition, the Wilson Tariff Act of 1894 (U.S. Code, Title 15, Sections 73-77) declares illegal, void, and punishable as a misdemeanor any combination, conspiracy, or contract, relating to the importation of goods into the United States, found to be "contrary to public policy." Any person found guilty of having violated this act is subject to a fine of up to $5,000 and a prison term not exceeding one year, as well as to a civil treble damage action brought by an individual harmed by the illegal action.

At the same time, a federal complaint may allege a violation of the Civil Rights Act of 1871. Section 1985(3) of Title 42 of the U.S. Code allows for the recovery of all damages resulting from the conspiracy by two or more persons, "for the purpose of depriving, either directly or indirectly, any person or class of persons of the equal protection of the laws, or of equal privileges and immunities under the laws. . . . " Section 1985(3) is well suited to fight those who submit to the Boycott's pressure in that no "state action" is required in order to come within its purview.

Similarly, the AJC's 1975 memorandum to the president suggested the implementation of the relevant provisions of the Federal Trade Commission Act, the Shipping Act, and the Federal Deposit Insurance Act, along with the promulgation of additional regulations thereunder, as additional federal legislative tools with which to counter the Boycott's activities.

The State commissions on discrimination, and the U.S. Equal Employment Opportunity Commission (EEOC), are other channels which may be utilized by individuals who have lost their jobs due to measures taken by the Arab Boycott. Concurrent with the filing of a complaint with the state commission on discrimination, one has the right to file a complaint before the EEOC, pursuant to Title VII of the Civil Rights Act of 1964. Such suits may result in the award of back pay and reinstatement and may, in some states, restitute the complainant for his mental suffering and loss of stature in his business and social community.

On July 29, 1975, a strong statement against employers who succumb to the Boycott's directives was issued by the Massachusetts Commission Against Discrimination (see Appendix E). Three months later, employers were warned by New York City's Commission on Human Rights not to discriminate against Jews after the commission had found "probable cause" in a complaint charging the American Oil Company (Amoco) with discrimination in the firing of a Jewish receptionist-typist whose job required the greeting of Arab visitors.[2]

At the same time, the New York State Banking Department warned all presidents of New York banks that state law forbids banks to discriminate on any basis:

> It has been reported that banks may be offered a substantial deposit or loan business from Arab countries subject to the condition that no member of the Jewish faith sit on the bank's board of directors or control any significant amount of the bank's stock. . . . Discriminatory practices or policies . . . have no place in the American heritage and are incompatible with the public service function of banking institutions in this state.[3]

In Massachusetts, as well as in many other states, the legislature has enacted a "Baby Federal Trade Commission Act." Chapter 93A of the Massachusetts

General Laws, as amended, allows a corporation or individual in business or
trade to sue another corporation or individual in commerce for perpetrating an
unfair or deceptive business or trade practice. The Massachusetts Supreme Judi-
cial Court has broadly interpreted this statute and there is a strong indication
that a person discharged due to his religion, race, or national origin, or a corporation omitted from a syndication due to its Jewish or pro-Israel officers or
board of directors, will be successful in an action brought pursuant to Chapter
93A. Similar to the antitrust laws, this statute allows for a recovery of treble
damages. However, it does not require proof of a conspiracy and affords the
state court discretion to award reasonable attorney fees and costs to the complainant who proves a willful violation of the statute. Finally, Chapter 93A
allows a plaintiff to join, in a class action, all people similarly affected by the
particular illegal act and he need not prove, as is necessary in the federal courts,
the superiority or predominance of a class action over separate actions brought
by individuals.

     In addition, the Anti-Defamation League has made excellent use of Execu-
tive Order 11246 and subsequent guidelines which "prohibit federal contractors
from discriminating on the basis of religion or national origin . . . when hiring for
work to be performed in the United States and abroad." Once the ADL submits
a complaint against a corporation alleging a pattern or practice of discrimination, on the grounds of religion or national origin, against U.S. citizens, the
federal agency responsible for the particular industry, trade, or commerce schedules a compliance review hearing. If the discrimination is found to exist, the
perpetrator of the misdeed must undertake affirmative action to recruit individuals of the same background of those against whom the initial discrimination
was practiced.

     Thus, the legal weapons already in existence with which to fight the
Boycott are numerous. A U.S. company guilty of complying with the Boycott
may be faced with the threat of concurrent suits in the federal and state courts
as well as in federal and state antidiscrimination agencies. Moreover, the publicity that such litigation engenders, more likely than not, will cause hearings to
take place before one or more congressional bodies, thereby increasing the
public's awareness of the alleged illegal acts. Thus, the mere threat of such anti-
Boycott action in the United States appears to be sufficiently formidable to
encourage most corporations to reject Arab Boycott solicitations.

     However, in contradistinction to the theoretical strength of the existing
anti-Boycott legislation, the combination of human frailty and corporate reality
must not be overlooked. Corporations dismissing Jews, or individuals with
Israeli origins, offer these former employees the "carrot" of excellent recommendations to future prospective employers, in exchange for silence on the subject of the Boycott. In general, a person concerned with his or her ability to earn
a living and support a family cannot be expected to wage a protracted legal
battle against a corporation. This is especially true given a lawyer's inability to

guarantee that the litigation will ultimately prove successful and be worth the effort. Although the Anti-Defamation League and the American Jewish Congress will offer their legal staffs and assistance funds to victims of the Arab Boycott, and private attorneys may take these matters pro bono, or on a contingency fee basis, an individual may find too difficult the monetary, temporal, and emotional demands required by such litigation.

Another plane of corporate reality relates to the manner in which Boycott pressures are concealed. A corporation may be approached privately, through letter, telephonic communication, or office conference. Most often, the Boycott does not seek the dismissal of an individual employee but, rather, the closing of an existing factory or agency is Israel, the termination of negotiations with an Israeli counterpart, or the mere promise not to do business in the future with Israel or with a Jewish company having strong ties with Israel. "Since there are a hundred legitimate reasons to switch from one supplier or contractor to another, how do we establish that a company is being frozen out because its owners or managers or professional staff are Jewish."[4] Clearly, this form of coercion will rarely rise to public awareness unless the solicited corporation desires, or is encouraged through external legal or economic means, to reveal that which was commenced through stealth.

Given these factors, we turn to those additional laws necessary in order to force the Boycott into the public arena, where it fares so poorly.

THE LAW—AS IT SHOULD BE

There is little doubt that Senator Williams is pursuing an important anti-Boycott course in his efforts (noted previously) to amend the Securities and Exchange Act of 1934. Yet, his amendment does not go far enough, since it only bars those foreign investors who force or attempt to force compliance with the Boycott from acquiring 5 percent or more of the corporate stock of an American concern. In order to successfully combat the Boycott, legislation must be passed which will bar (1) any investment whatsoever in the United States by those Arab governments, companies, or individuals who aid and abet the Boycott; and (2) any business relationship whatsoever established with U.S. companies and financial institutions by those foreign corporations or individuals who act as agents for, or comply with, Boycott demands. The first of these requirements is necessary to indicate to the Arabs that they cannot expect to invest within the United States if they are pursuing a policy harmful to an ally of the United States and to American citizens of the Jewish faith or of Israeli national origin.

The second clause is necessary to deal with the Kleinwort, Benson situation (described previously). Kleinwort, Benson, and those companies operating in similar fashion, should no longer be allowed to effect exclusive or cooperative financings in the United States, given their willingness to react favorably to Arab

Boycott demands. Thus, the choice confronting these companies should not be one between the Arab and Israeli markets but, rather, between Arab business and the consumptive capacity of the United States.

Similarly, there is a need for legislation relating to domestic companies that succumb to the dictates of the Boycott. Senator Williams's bill, which passed the Senate Banking Committee on December 17, 1975, would, inter alia, prohibit American firms from refusing to do business with other U.S. companies because of Boycott demands and would insure public disclosure of Boycott overtures and the names of companies complying with Boycott requests.[5]

In addition, however, severe sanctions, including a mandatory minimum fine of $50,000 upon individuals and $500,000 upon corporations, should be added to the Export Administration Act with regard to those who fail to promptly supply the information sought by the Commerce Department. Likewise the Holtzman-Rodino legislation, which would impose fines and/or imprisonment upon companies or executives who assist in Boycott activities or comply with Boycott demands, must be acted upon positively by Congress and signed into law by the president. Such civil and criminal penalties are urgently needed to augment and strengthen all existing and future legislation. Although the secrecy of Boycott approaches cannot be prevented, the incremented risks of compliance will counterbalance the strictly-business approach afforded the Boycott agents heretofore.

Congress should give serious consideration to (1) Congressman Drinan's foreign discriminatory practices bill of 1975, which includes provisions to revoke the export licenses of those who comply directly or indirectly with the Boycott, and allows for individual civil actions seeking injunctive and monetary relief against such pro-Boycott forces; (2) the Williams-Schweiker suggestion that the president, hereafter, must justify to Congress and, hence, to the American public, any continuation of foreign aid or military sales to countries practicing discrimination against American citizens or who attempt to tamper with the free market of American business interrelationships within and without the United States; (3) Senator Kennedy's proposal that the government should reconsider its guarantees of private investments in Saudi Arabia in view of that country's blacklist and Boycott policy; (4) a suggestion that Title 42, Section 1983, of the U.S. Code be amended to allow individuals and corporations to sue American companies acting "under color of" foreign, as well as state or territorial law, and who, in furtherance of Boycott demands, deprive a U.S. citizen or corporation of the rights, privileges, and immunities secured by the Constitution and other federal and state laws; and (5) specific additions to the federal and state banking and investment company statutes which would forbid and punish compliance with the Boycott (this legislation would prove to be unnecessary if the Williams-Schweiker, Williams-Javits, Stevenson, Drinan, and Holtzman bills were passed).

More important than all legislation, however, is the issuance of a clear and forceful statement, by the president of the United States and the secretary of state, placing the Arab nations on notice that the economic crossroad has been reached and a choice must be made: either do business with all Americans or do business with none; no constitutional, statutory, or common law right of an American individual or corporation will be abridged.

NOTES

1. Jerusalem *Post*, January 19, 1976.

2. Jerusalem *Post*, September 18, 1975. In February 1976, public hearings on the Arab Boycott were held by New York State's Assembly Subcommittee on Human Rights. The Subcommittee's chairman, Assemblyman Joseph F. Lisa, declared: "New York State ... will continue to show the nation how to combat the discriminatory boycotts." Press Release (mimeographed), from the office of Assemblyman Joseph F. Lisa, New York State Assembly, Albany, New York, January 28, 1976.

3. New York *Post*, May 13, 1975.

4. Bertram H. Gold, "Americans Against Americans: Playing the Arab Game," *Hadassah Magazine*, June 1975, p. 9. In March 1976, it was reported that Rastum Bastuni, an ex-member of the Israeli Knesset, who had left Israel for the United States and had joined the New York architectural firm of Rogers, Butter and Bergen, had been dismissed by the firm as a result of Arab Boycott pressures. Rogers, Butter and Bergen, at the same time, allegedly dismissed its two remaining Jewish employees in an attempt to solicit Arab orders for architectural services regarding a large hospital project in Cairo, among others. *Omer* 2, no. 1 (Israel: daily newspaper, March 21, 1976).

5. Jerusalem *Post*, December 19, 1975.

THE JEWISH ORGANIZATIONS

As we have seen, the main organizations that assume active and coordinated anti-Boycott stances within the Jewish community are the Anti-Defamation League of B'nai B'rith and the American Jewish Congress (AJC). In the instances in which the ADL and/or the AJC have given wide publicity to a particular corporate or governmental compliance with the Boycott, their successes have been admirable. Moreover, where there has been an indication that a corporation has succumbed to Boycott demands, the ADL and/or the AJC through quiet diplomacy, often have been able to "cajole" the corporation either to adopt a neutral stance whereby it deals both with Israel and the Arab countries, or to totally reject the Arab overtures.

Similarly, the America-Israel Public Affairs Committee (AIPAC), based in Washington, has exposed and attacked the Boycott in its publication, *Near East Report.* Along with AIPAC, the American Jewish Committee (the committee) has assumed an important role through its support of anti-Boycott legislation and the exertion of public and private anti-Boycott pressures.[1]

However, the ADL, the AJC, AIPAC, and the committee, until the period following the 1973 Yom Kippur War, have been hampered by Israel's official policy which discouraged well-publicized and spirited combat against Boycott caprices. To some extent, one might view these organizations as having internalized this Israeli position. Furthermore, these organizations have been beset with budgetary and manpower problems which have rendered them incapable of responding to the Boycott in a forceful and fully effective manner. Finally, although Executive Order 11246 (the contract compliance procedure) has been utilized successfully by ADL counsel, until 1975 most existing laws rarely, if

74

ever have been implemented and employed to fight the Boycott, and lobbying and public pressure for more effectual counter-Boycott legislation has been weak.

Now, however, AIPAC, the ADL, the AJC, and the committee, adopting a united front, are entering the struggle against the Boycott. A positive commitment has been made to actively publicize the Boycott and support the new Drinan-Holtzman-Williams legislation. It is expected that, as a result of this concerted effort, a new public awareness of the Boycott and its insidious role in international and American economic affairs will emerge.

Clearly, publicity is the key in this united action. A brochure on the Boycott will be prepared for mass distribution. This brochure will contain, in an abridged form, all information necessary for an individual to understand the full panoply of Boycott activities and how one can assume an active anti-Boycott role.

In addition, there are plans to publish a *Boycott Alert Bulletin,* to be distributed on a monthly basis, with supplements when necessary. This bulletin will be distributed to members of the Jewish community, as well as to senators, congressmen, assemblymen, lay and religious leaders of all faiths, and to the news media. An international version of this bulletin may be published as well. In addition, articles on the Boycott will appear periodically and the nature of corporate compliance with the Boycott will be reported quarterly.

The purpose of this publicity, however, cannot be solely to inform the public about the Boycott, although this is an important goal. The public must be encouraged to counter the Boycott's influence and efforts and, as will be shown in the following section, the public arena is where the battle against the Boycott will be successfully waged.

Further, companies in particular industries must be shown that a united rejection of Boycott demands has succeeded, historically, in forcing the Boycott authorities to back down. Discrimination is too high a price to pay for an Arab market that needs the highly efficient technology of the United States, and its highly productive service industries, a great deal more than American companies need the Arab market. The Arabs have used their "trump card"—oil. It is time to call their bluff.

Finally, as Chaim Herzog has suggested, it has become necessary to convene a World Economic Conference "to devise an answer to the Arab Boycott and those who submit to it, and mobilize . . . support for those who oppose Arab blackmail."[2] This conference will act as the germinating source of ideas and effective action and, perhaps, will establish regional, national, and international anti-Boycott centers of activity. Two such centers of activity are Jerusalem, where Avraham Agmon heads the Finance Ministry's anti-Boycott unit, and New York, where Edgar Bronfman has been named by the World Jewish Congress as chairman of a seven-man committee to coordinate the fight against the Boycott.[3]

COMMUNAL AND INDIVIDUAL RESPONSE

The planned *Boycott Alert Bulletin* must advise the Jewish community, public officials, and the American public, of the names of those domestic and foreign companies currently complying with the Boycott and, just as important, those companies rejecting all Boycott overtures. Certainly, one must view as unforgivable the fact that American families, in ignorance of certain companies' pro-Boycott activities, purchase such companies' products. It is not important to place the blame for this ignorance. The want of knowledge, however, must be remedied at once.

A useful manner in which individuals may exert pressure upon a company complying with the Boycott is through the purchase of a small amount of the common stock and attendance at the company's annual meetings, whereat questions relating to Boycott complicity may be aired. At the same time, a stockholder list should be obtained and letters may be sent to the shareholders of record, describing the pro-Boycott activities of the company. Such a company will be given a period in which to purge itself of the stigma of Boycott complicity. Threats of counter-Boycott measures, including picketing, will be adopted if a satisfactory resolution of the controversy is not reached.

In December 1975, the AJC recognized the usefulness of the stock purchase method. The congress purchased five shares of stock in five selected companies—the General Motors Corporation, the Hewlett-Packard Company, the International Harvester Company, Texaco, Inc., and World Airways, Inc.—and announced that it would introduce stockholder resolutions at these companies' annual meetings in order to force companies to disclose any involvement in the Arab Boycott of Israel. Members of the AJC who are shareholders in these companies have volunteered to sponsor the respective resolutions, and the AJC hopes, eventually, to use such resolutions against more than one hundred leading American companies.[4] However, the AJC should recall that the medium-size and small companies are most vulnerable to the Boycott's demands and that many of the so-called leading American companies have been blacklisted by the Arabs.

In addition to the stockholder activities described above, it is expected that the general public shall vigorously support those companies presently on the Boycott's blacklist. There is every reason for the public, Jews and non-Jews alike, to give business to blacklisted concerns, until their competitors "join" the blacklist, thereby effectively rejecting the Boycott's policy. Similarly, if an individual engineer or architect is victimized by the Boycott, firms in the vicinity will be expected to hire these women and men.

The blacklist must be used, through public outcry, as a tool in the ultimate destruction of the Boycott. Companies, ships, and individuals will be encouraged to have their names inscribed on the blacklist, thereby undercutting whatever leverage the acts of blacklisting may have upon those who are approached by the Boycott and its agents. Advertisements by large companies, such as Xerox,

Zenith, General Tire, and Chemstrand, should appear in newspapers throughout the country announcing: "We are on the Arab Blacklist—Join Us!" A similar, intraindustry, advertisement should be prepared by those companies, within a particular industry, that find themselves on the blacklist (for example, Zenith, RCA, and Motorola; or M. C. Shoe, Fortune Shoe, and Sovereign Shoe).

The message will be a simple one and will be directed not only to those who have complied, or plan to comply, with the Boycott but, also, to those who have resisted such approaches. The Arabs do not have a monopoly on the use of economic power.[5]

NOTES

1. The American Jewish Committee has pursued a more silent approach in combating the Arab Boycott. Little is read in the daily press of the committee's activities. Yet, as seen in an article appearing in *Hadassah Magazine* in June 1975, written by the committee's executive vice president, Bertram H. Gold, the committee has moved swiftly and effectively against acts of discrimination. In 1975, the Defense Department retained the Vinnell Corporation, an American company, to train a new Saudi Arabian National Guard. In the initial draft of the written agreement between the department and Vinnell, the standard anti-discrimination clause that, by law, must be part of every government contract was omitted. The clause "was put back only when the American Jewish Committee raised Cain about it." p. 29.

2. Jerusalem *Post Weekly*, March 25, 1975.

3. Jerusalem *Post Weekly,* May 20, 1975.

4. New York *Times,* December 3, 1975. In November 1975, the General Electric Corporation (GE), in federal court, sought to bar a state legislative committee from issuing a subpoena for its records for its transactions with Arab customers. GE's action was taken due to the "substantial injury" that may result to the corporation as a result of "press distortions." Jerusalem *Post,* November 20, 1975. Federal District Court Judge James T. Foley denied GE's motion for a preliminary injunction and GE has appealed this decision to the U.S. Court of Appeals for the Second Circuit. Albany *Times Union,* January 14, 1976. In all fairness to GE, however, it should be noted that, at the present time, the company does more business with Israel than with all Arab countries combined.

In March 1976, the American Jewish Congress supported a federal suit filed by Mr. and Mrs. Martin K. Balter against Eastman Kodak Co. The suit sought to prevent Kodak from holding its annual meeting in April 1976 on the grounds that Kodak refused to include in its proxy papers the Balter's proposed resolution, which would require Kodak to report company policy regarding any meeting. Jerusalem *Post*, March 28, 1976.

5. Excellent evidence of this nascent countereconomic power are the thousands of hotel reservation cancellations in Mexico and Brazil following the anti-Zionist vote in the United Nations in late 1975. See for example *Jorno do Brasil,* January 6, 1976. In March 1976, the American Jewish Congress announced that it had received written assurances from 22 of the largest corporations in the United States (including General Motors, RCA, and Texaco) that they would not submit to Arab Boycott demands. Jerusalem *Post*, March 17, 1976.

6

THE FUTURE: DREAMS, STRATEGY, AND REALITY

THE ROLE OF ARAB OIL

Although many Arab countries have one-commodity economies, this single commodity, oil, has accelerated their transition from tradition-oriented to burgeoning, modern societies and has placed them in a position of economic and political power. Due to this power, it is safe to assume that the Arabs hope to continue their Boycott of Israel indefinitely, regardless of "any action taken by the United Nations, the World Court or the big powers."[1]

This dream of shattering Israel's economy is premised on the following assumptions: that Middle East oil will maintain its dominant status in world markets for years to come; that Israel will not be able to withstand future Boycott activities in the manner in which she has withstood such pressures in the past; and that the Boycott's effectiveness can, and will, be increased.

These assumptions, however, have extremely fragile foundations. With an oil boom looming imminent in Mexico, Canada, Alaska, Russia, and the North Sea, concurrent with an apparent surge in technological research relating to alternate sources of energy, one may question the future economic viability of the Middle East's oil supply.

Moreover, Israel now has recognized the importance of combatting the Arab Boycott. In conjunction with this recognition is the world Jewish community's willingness to unite its efforts to offset and counter Boycott pressures. These factors augur ill for the assumption that Israel will be unable to withstand future Boycott pressures. The Boycott's effectiveness will decrease in inverse proportion to the increase in public awareness of its activities and the methods by which the Boycott's efforts may be rendered nugatory.

For a boycott to be successful, many factors must exist and coalesce. The boycotting party must have "a strong and widespread sense of injury and injustice"[2] and a "concrete expression of principle,"[3] providing an emotional issue toward which Arabs may rally. Although the Arab League's activities, and to some extent the Palestinian issue, have provided this rallying point,[4] the Arab nations have been unable to produce the unified commitment necessary to make the Boycott a success. Thus, we have seen how the Maghreb nations (Morocco, Algeria, and Tunisia), along with Lebanon, have shown little enthusiasm toward implementing Boycott resolutions. In fact, the Arab League, in general, has reechoed the following historical tradition: except for the 1973-74 oil embargo, the Arabs have displayed a persistent inability to unite either politically or economically.[5]

A boycott also will be more likely to succeed if the boycotting countries hold a "unique complementary relationship to the boycotted nation."[6] Yet, Israel has been able to receive oil from Iran and, between 1967 and 1975, from the Abu Rhudeis fields, and has found Western sources for her essential goods and Western markets for her exports, thereby becoming independent of the Arab economies.

Finally, in order for a boycott to attain its objectives, it must not only have the financial means to sustain sanctions for a long period of time but must be relatively harmless to those who implement the boycott policies. Yet, as in the cases (described previously) of Hilton, Coca Cola, the Chase Manhattan Bank, and the Ford Motor Company, the rules promulgated by the Boycott Office have been changed frequently, and often radically, in order to avoid financial chaos in the Arab business community. The Ford case presents an excellent example:

> To have closed the Alexandria assembly plant while the Moroccans continued to build trucks for the Arab world would have hurt the United Arab Republic [Egypt] more than Israel. Parts for Ford trucks already operating in the Arab world would have been more difficult to obtain, and many distributors and dealers whose lifetime had been devoted to building a Ford market would have been lost.[7]

Similarly, the Arabs do business with IBM, yet tourists visiting Jerusalem may readily observe the IBM sign, in Hebrew, on Keren Hayesod Street.

The *Middle East Economic Digest,* a British publication sympathetic to the Arab cause, observed "evidence of a new and flexible approach" toward the Boycott on the part of certain Arab countries:

> Both Egypt and Syria are bringing forward proposals that companies could be lifted from the "Black List" if they contribute to the economic development of the Arab world to a greater degree than their involvement in Israel. The Egyptian proposal calls for an involvement in Egypt to a value of at least twice as much capital as is invested in any Israeli operations. The Syrian proposal calls for

setting up commercial operations which should be at least compa-
rable to any ventures in Israel. Such operations could be part-
financed with Arab capital. Some reports suggest that three times
the value of a company's Israeli operations will be required.[8]

The *Arab Economist,* too, recognized an "important proviso" to the Boycott policy currently practiced by the countries comprising the Arab League:
"Blacklisting will not be applied whenever the overall result or results will be
more detrimental to Arab economies than to Israel's."[9]

Upon a review of the Arab League's Boycott and its effect on world trade,
it seems evident that, instead of expending their energies on a destructive boycott the Arabs should

> use the technical experience which the Israelis have gained; . . . [and]
> cooperate in the development of water resources in the Middle East.
> . . . In their own interest, it is time for the Arabs to reexamine the
> whole concept of the boycott of Israel.[10]

Today, however, this observation clearly is but a dream. Given the present
Middle East crisis, the Arabs feel obligated to continue their economic Boycott
of Israel.

A penultimate word of caution is in order. The Boycott has not been the
major source of Israel's recent economic and financial problems and Israel
should avoid using the Boycott as its economic scapegoat. "The end of the boycott will not constitute that hoped-for miracle which is to take the place of the
fundamental reorganization of economic life which is held to be necessary if
Israel is to become self-supporting."[11] Although Israel has commenced this
"fundamental reorganization," we must remember that only through continued
industrial development and expansion, and its achievement of product superiority in all endeavors, will it attain economic viability in world markets. An
excellent first step was the comprehensive new trade agreement, providing for
the gradual elimination of all protective tariffs between Israel and the European
Common Market, that went into effect on July 1, 1975.[12] The Parliament of
Europe, meeting in Strasbourg in December 1975, further softened certain regulations relating to Israeli access to the European economic union and agreed to
work for the expansion of financial, industrial, and technological ties between
the European Economic Community and Israel. The Parliament, too, voted to
send a delegation to visit Israel in May 1976.[13]

Of equal importance may be the U.S.-Israel Economic Agreement of May
1975. This agreement provides for the expansion of economic cooperation between the two countries in the fields of trade, investments, raw materials, and
research and development, and includes a statement opposing "restrictive trade
practices or boycotts against countries friendly to either."[14]

In conclusion, the Arab Boycott, in its primary, secondary, and tertiary form, represents a serious danger to the free international market conditions regarded by Israel and the world as all-important for economic cooperation and expansion. Although the large corporations are capable of dealing with the Boycott, corporations of lesser size are more likely to yield to the Boycott's pressure unless public awareness and legal sanctions are augmented. Israel and the United States, in conjunction with fair-minded governments, corporations, individuals, and Jewish communal organizations throughout the world should, and indeed must, engage the Arab Boycott in the complexities of economic and legal warfare, and emerge triumphant.

NOTES

1. New York *Times* (international edition), June 14, 1959.

2. A. R. C. De Crispigny and R. T. McKinnell, "The Nature and Significance of Economic Boycott," *The South African Journal of Economics* (December 1960):23.

3. Pierre Roudot, "Arab Boycott as Myth," *New Outlook* 6, no. 5 (June 1963): 23.

4. "[O]ne of the principal benefits of the Boycott's program in the Arab League's eyes is that it keeps the issue of Israel constantly before the Arab people." Robert W. MacDonald, *The League of Arab States: A Study in the Dynamics of Regional Organization* (Princeton, N.J.: Princeton University Press, 1965), p. 119.

5. This rather broad generalization is given some substantiation by the following statements: (1) "As an expression of unity, the [Arab] League was faint and feeble." F. Sayegh, *Arab Unity: Hope and Fulfillment* (London: Devin Publishers, 1958), p. 8; (2) "[T]he League failed completely to move a single step forward along the path of political integration but rather proved to be 'an instrument of the status quo.'" N. Izzedin, *The Arab World,* 1953, p. 324; both cited in M. F. Anatwabi, *Arab Unity in Terms of Law* (The Hague: Martinus Nijhoff, 1963), p. 165. It should be added that, although the Council of Arab Economic Unity was established on June 6, 1962, and this council, on August 13, 1964, announced the creation of the Arab Common Market, few economic benefits have resulted from these actions. See Anatwabi, ibid.

6. Robert E. Weigand, "The Arab League Boycott of Israel," *Michigan State University Business Topics* (Spring 1968):77.

7. Ibid.

8. *Middle East Economic Digest,* August 22, 1975, p. 3.

9. *Arab Economist,* "The Boycott of Isreal Office," (April 1975):36.

10. *Spectator* (London), April 15, 1960.

11. Gardner Patterson, "Israel's Economic Problems," *Foreign Affairs* 32, no. 2 (January 1954): 322, cited in Oded Remba, "The Arab Boycott: A Study in Total Economic Warfare," *Midstream* 6, no. 3 (Summer 1960): 51.

12. New York *Times,* May 8, 1975.

13. *Maariv,* December 19, 1975; Jerusalem *Post,* December 23, 1975.

14. Jerusalem *Post Weekly,* May 20, 1975.

THE AFFIDAVIT

A firm doing business in the Arab world for the first time must have a corporate officer sign a notarized affidavit that it does not, and will not, violate Boycott regulations. A sample follows:

We hereby, certify under our own responsibility, that our firm, namely, _____, has no commercial, industrial, and/or any other relations with Israel; our firm does not constitute a branch, subsidiary, or main office of any other Israeli firm. We further declare that we have no direct or indirect interests in all or any Israeli concerns, whether governmental or nongovernmental.

THE CERTIFICATE OF ORIGIN

Firms shipping goods to Arab countries must provide a negative certificate of origin. The following is a sample from the San Francisco Chamber of Commerce:

I hereby certify that I have investigated the foregoing statements and to the best of my knowledge and belief the articles described above are the growth, product, or manufacture of the United States of America; furthermore that these articles are not of Israeli origin, and that no Israeli products were used in their manufacture.

THE QUESTIONNAIRE

Firms suspected of dealing with Israel receive a questionnaire from the Central Boycott Office in Damascus demanding private information and assurance that trade with Israel will be discontinued. A sample questionnaire follows:

Gentlemen:

We wish to inform you that we have acquired reliable information to the effect that you are the agents of the X.Y.Z. Company of Israel.

In this regard, we believe that it is of mutual interest to both of us to draw your attention to the fact that the Arab countries are still in a state of war with Israel. Therefore, as a measure of self-defense and with a view to safeguarding the rights and vital interests of the Arabs of Palestine, the Arab countries strictly adhere to a set of boycott rules directed at Israel. . . . Violation of these regulations entails the boycott of violators in the Arab countries.

However, before any action is taken against your firm, we find it beneficial for you, as well as for us, to contact you directly so that you may inform us of the nature of the dealings of your firm with Israel. This will have to be done in the form of a declaration duly signed before the competent governmental authorities and should also bear a final authentication to the signature of the authorized representative of your firm appended thereto by the closest consulate or diplomatic mission of any Arab country. The required declaration will have to contain complete answers to the following questions:

1) Do you have any branch, office, or agency in Israel? In case you have, please state the nature of its activity.

2) Do you act as general agents of Israeli companies? Particularly, the X.Y.Z. company of Israel.

3) Have you ever owned shares in Israeli firms or businesses?

4) Is your firm or any of its directors a member of any foreign-Israeli chamber of commerce in Israel or abroad?

If your answer is in the positive, you will then be kindly requested to present the following:

a) An official copy of your agency agreement with the said company [other Israeli company], provided that it be duly certified by your chamber of commerce in writing and authenticated by your competent governmental authorities and by any Arab consulate in your area of activity.

b) Documentation to the effect that you have terminated the agency agreement and showing the consent of the Israeli side to such termination. Such documents will have to be duly certified as shown in the above paragraph.

c) An undertaking to the effect that you will never represent Israeli companies in the future.

We look forward to receiving your reply in the above-mentioned form within a maximum period not to exceed three months from the date of this letter.

Finally, we do hope that you will extend sympathetic under-standing of the compelling considerations which render these measures mandatory. It is our sincere hope that you will find it appropriate to maintain your commercial relations with the Arab countries.

Very truly yours,

Mohammed Mahmoud Mahgoub
Commissioner General,
Central Office for the
Boycott of Israel

VIEW I*

Any attempt to explain definitely the boycotting procedure is doomed to failure because of (a) the general unpredictability of the Central Boycott Office; (b) the autonomy of the regional (i.e., national) boycott offices; (c) the dual authority (between the Central Boycott Office and the regional offices) to initiate inquiries and investigations; and (d) the uncertain status of decisions reached by the regional boycott officers conferences. Any statements made in this section, therefore, must be treated as *generalizations*; exceptions to any of them can usually be found.

Most Boycott actions begin in the Central Boycott Office (CBO) in Damascus, though any regional office may independently and without CBO approval begin its own inquiry. Also, an Arab firm may ask a supplier (or potential supplier) to respond to the usual boycott office questions, so as to avoid entering into contractual relations with a firm that might later be boycotted. Little is known about the sources of information that trigger CBO or other inquiries; they may be reports from Arab embassies, trade and financial journals, Israeli and Zionist publications, or even malicious gossip from a firm's competitor or a disgruntled employee. Whatever the reason, a letter or inquiry [see Appendix A] is sent to the firm or the firm's agent, and a period of time, usually three months, is fixed for the firm to deny the charges or take steps to terminate the relationship in question.

If the first letter is not answered, a warning letter is sent. Failure to respond is, in effect, considered to be admission of guilt, and the firm is usually recommended for blacklisting. It is not clear whether all such cases are first considered by the semi-annual regional boycott officers conference or whether the CBO can recommend blacklisting in some cases on its own authority.

If a firm decides to respond to either letter, its response must normally be in the form of a notarized statement, authenticated by an Arab consular official. Until recently, authentication by the Department of State was also required (by

---

*The following is taken verbatim from James H. Bahti, *The Arab Economic Boycott of Israel* (Washington, D.C.: The Brookings Institution, 1967), pp. 11-14. The author wishes to thank Mr. Bahti for his permission to present his interpretation of the boycotting procedure.

the Arab consular officials, not the CBO), but the Department no longer authenticates documents having to do with boycott matters. The firm may, for example, deny the charges, present a correct version of the charges, or, admitting the charges, claim that there has been no violation of the boycott regulations. Such a response usually involves answers to the "standards" questionnaire. On occasion, firms have taken offense at the letter of inquiry and replied with a critical or sarcastic letter. In such cases, Congressmen and the Departments of State and Commerce may also receive letters of protest from the offended firm.

If the CBO is satisfied with the response, the matter is dropped. Often, however, the CBO will send follow-up inquiries, requesting additional proof, explanations, or copies of documents, and the entire procedure can become burdensome and expensive. Some inquiries have taken well over a year to complete, and then, after a short period, the whole inquiry is re-initiated. Dilatory tactics by a firm, even when resigned to eventual boycotting, can drag out the procedure for months or even years. In addition to using correspondence, firms have been known to have their local agents argue on their behalf, or company officials may visit the boycott authorities to present their cases.

Once the CBO has assembled its documentation, the case is raised at the regional boycott officers conference. The conference may (a) withdraw the charges against the firm, (b) recommend that the firm be boycotted, or (c) recommend further study, e.g., a case involving a financial institution might require the advice of Arab banking authorities.

The decisions of the conference are then communicated to the Arab League member states as well as to those Arab political units that are not members of the League but which support the boycott.

VIEW II*

Banning

Once it becomes established to any of the individual offices that a firm or individual have contravened the Boycott rules the case is thereupon referred to the Headquarters (in Damascus) which examines the information and issues a warning to the offender. The usual grace period for compliance with the warning is three months but the actual period could be made longer subject to factors governing each case. Should the offender fail to regularize his position then the Head Office (Headquarters) may solicit the opinions of each Arab country's boycott office on the case under examination. Should the majority concur and in

---

*The following is taken verbatim from "The Boycott of Israel Office," *Arab Economist* (Beirut), April 1975, p. 36 ff.

the absence of any proposal that the matter be arbitrated in a Boycott conference the ban will be considered as having been imposed by the most recent conference. Such will then be communicated to the regional offices by the Head Office and the ban goes into effect.

Charges brought against an offender are to be verified prior to action by reliable authorities, preferably Arab embassies or equivalent organizations like joint committees. In the absence of firm evidence the company(ies) concerned may be asked to establish verified proof of their noninvolvement which then will be referred to the regional office which brought up the charge in the first place.

Lifting a Ban

Generally the rules applying to imposing bans apply also to their lifting. An application to lift off a ban may be made to any regional office upon which it is relayed immediately to the Head Office. It is then examined and relayed to all other regional offices for their stance and comments. Should the majority agree to the proposal of lifting the ban and, in the absence of any objection based on fundamental reasons requiring that the subject by acted upon in a conference (of all regional boycott offices) the ban lifting application will be considered as having been approved by the most recently held conference.

Papers and documents submitted in support of applications to lift a ban must be verified by chambers of commerce or labor unions, or they must be affirmed by duly appointed notaries public in the country of origin. Such documents must also be validated and confirmed by Arab embassies in the country concerned.

The procedure of imposing or lifting a ban through a decision by the Boycott Head Office is exceptional. It is intended to expedite decisions. But questions of broader significance such as those pertaining to arms companies, petroleum firms and monopoly concessionaires have to be handled in a general conference only or by the unanimous decision of each and every regional office—a full consensus.

Who Imposes or Lifts Bans?

The Boycott Office is not a state within a state. Its functions are strictly advisory. The decision to impose or lift a ban is made by the political authorities such as the Council of Ministers in Lebanon. Thus it is conceivable that a firm may be ostracized in one country and transacted with by another.

KAWASAKI DOCKYARD CO., LTD.
14 Higashi-Kawasaki-Cho
2-Chome
Ikuta-ku, Kobe, Japan

Our File No. KMB-67-10291

Kobe, July 6, 1967

Mr. E. Epstein
Representative
Zim Israel Navigation Co., Ltd.
C/o Sannomiya Bldg.,
<u>KOBE</u>

<u>Re: Abt. 100,000 DWT Oil Tanker</u>

Dear Sir:

With regard to the subject matter, it is our real regret to inform you by this letter that we have to decline this new building deal on the ground of the following aspects for all of our various negotiations with you until this very day.

Namely, one of the Kawasaki Group company has a business transaction with the U.A.R. which fact was not made known to us at the time of our early negotiation with you for this deal. However, this fact has been recently put before us at a consultation meeting of the Kawasaki Group and at that meeting, the said company has strongly made his appeal to us that we discontinue this particular business for Israel.

Under the above circumstances, we, all of a sudden are compelled to put forward this declination to you with a thousand pities and this matter will trouble our conscience for your very kind assistance made in negotiation this deal to date. Please understand our position and accept our deep apology for this unhappy situation.

Taking this opportunity, we wish to add that this action has no bearing with the Japanese government and we have never received their instruction nor suggestion and the decisions made by us is purely based on our discretion.

We trust that this declination will not have any unfavourable influence on our amicable relations with your esteemed company.

Yours very truly,

KAWASAKI   DOCKYARD   CO.,   LTD.

s/Y Madono
Manager
Marine Business Section

SHIBA ELECTRIC CO., LTD.

Our Reference No. 1434

Messrs. M. Schweiger
POP 4368
  Haifa
  Israel   Tokyo, 15th May 1967

Dear Sirs:

Subject: Closed Circuit Television

Thanks for your kind letter dated 7 May 1967 for the subject.

In this regard, to our regret, we wish to refrain from quoting the article, because our company have closely dealt with Arabic countries.

Please understand our position as above.

Yours faithfully,

Shiba Electric Co., Ltd.

M. Takekawa
Manager of Overseas Dept.

MARUSEI BOEKI CO., LTD.
Manufacturer & Exporter

Cable Address: Tel: (861) 4451,
"SANMARUI" TOKYO   No. 22 - 3, 2 Chome,   4452, 4453,
    Codes Used   Yanagibashi, Daito-Ku,   4454.
Bentley's; Acme   TOKYO, JAPAN

                                                    No. _____
                                                    Tokyo,   May 15, 1967

MESSRS. B.A.T. Trading Co., LTD.
P.O. Box 3341, Jerusalem,
Israel

Gentlemen:

Following up to our letter of May 13, as we have enclosed our Sales Note of #BT-2019 and imformed you that in our actuall shipment will be done under the term of F.O.B. Japan. And all of the goods shall be shipped in our due course. However, unfortunatelly hereafter we have to have another problem here. At the end of last week, we were visited by our customer from BEIROUT who is our old customer taking care of THE AREA OF ARABIAN COUNTRIES. And during his stay in Japan we asked him the import situation in that Area. And then we got the answer that if we export our goods to your country, we are to be boycotted by the government from that area.

As far as such market situation is concerned, we cannot export our goods to your country under our company name. We didn't recognize this kinds of problem not to export under our name. So far, as long as were are obliged into this kinds of problem against the government of that area, we have to take another way for your market.

And therefore we are very sorry to offer you our products without imformation for the solution of this kinds of problem. So we are pleased to imform you our got idea to solute this problem herein.

Here is one of our brother company named AZUMA TOY MFG. CO., who can handle our products under the same condition and terms. And so if you don't mind to import about this kinds of toys products from them, we can take care of your importation under the name of AZUMA TOYS MFG. This is the only solution of this kinds of problem which we can import our products to your market. We are very very sure that we can handle our products under the same terms and conditions as our handling under the name of AZUMA TOYS MFG.

And so we have to ask you again your same L/C of US$358.22 under the name of AZUMA TOYS MFG., and then we can ship the same goods of "FUJI PRESS" products. And when you shall establish another L/C of $358.22 under the name of AZUMA TOYS MFG., please note that the term should be noted CIF EILAT, not F.O.B. JAPAN. And this L/C of E.86268 is to be returned to you. And we will cover the whole charge which you spent when you establish this L/C, so please let us know your charge amount which you spent for banking in the same time when you shall get the details for another L/C of US$358.22 named AZUMA TOYS MFG:

In our future communication should be done to the following stated name:
MESSRS. AZUMA TOYS MFG.,
No. 21, 4-CHOME, KURAMAE, DAITO-KU, TOKYO, JAPAN

After receipt of your revised L/C for "FUJI PRESS" toys, we will make our Sales Note and imform you our shipping schedule.

We are very very sorry that we gave you so many troubles and confusable jobs; however, we are very lucky that we can get the solution before we shall ship our products to you.

In the future correspondence to AZUMA TOYS MFG., we will know every things our future business, and we can offer you through AZUMA TOYS MFG.

We are expecting for your kind and prompt cooperation for the above matter and your early reply is highly appreciated; we are,

Very truly yours,

MARUSEI BOEKI CO., LTD.

J. NOMATO

Wafa Wa Amal Society

P.O. Box 120   Cairo Egypt

Cairo, February 10, 1975

Gentlemen,

This is to enquire of your interest in being considered for appointment as Architect-Engineers for the Wafa Wa Amal Hospital and Rehabilitation Center in Cairo, Egypt. It comes to you, and a small number of other firms, on our understanding of your expereince in design of medical facilities. If you are interested in being considered, we request that you submit the qualifications of your firm and other information required by the enclosed terms of reference.

This information, which will constitute a proposal for professional services, should be in the hands of the Society by 2 P.M. March 20, 1975. Your proposal should be addressed to:

General Dr. Hassan Hosni,
Medical Director,
Wafa Wa Amal Center
P.O. Box 120,
Cairo, Egypt

By the act of submitting a proposal, the proposer declares he does not possess any plant, firm or branch in Israel, that he does not participate in any firm or company established in Israel, and he has not any supply, manufacturing, assembling, license or technical assistance agreement with any firm, company or person established or resident in Israel.

The proposer further undertakes not to have either by himself or through an intermediary any such activity in Israel and not to contribute in any to consolidate the economy or military efforts of Israel.

The proposal should be English.

From information submitted by invited firms, three or four firms will be selected for interview. On the basis of the total information available to the Society, one of the interviewed firms will be appointed as Architect-Engineer.

All correspondence concerning the project should be addressed to the Board of the Wafa Wa Amal Society through General, Dr. Hassan Hosni.

Very truly yours,

For the Board
General, Dr. Hassan Hosni

Ministry of Education

Tender No.: MA/30/75-76
Lab Equipment for Physics Dept.
Closing Date: June 15, 1975

Terms and Conditions:

1) Prices nett, CIF Kuwait, which should be firm for a period of 90 days from the closing date of the tender.

2) Goods offered should be exact to tender specifications and deviations, if any, should be made quite clear.

3) *Shipment*: Shipment must be effected within 60/75 days, in case of an order.

4) State name of the manufacturers and their address.

5) Bid Bond 2% of the total value valid for 90 days from the closing date of the tender, in favour of the Central Tenders Committee, and if succeeded, Performance Guarantee for 10% of the order value, valid for the complete period of delivery, plus another 3 months to cover penalty for late delivery due to causes other than bonafide force-majeure are required.

   Note: – We can arrange these guarantees on your behalf in good faith assuming when you have made an offer you will not fail to fulfil your obligations due to reasons other than bonafide force-majeure conditions.

6) Ministry reserves the right to increase or decrease the quantity up to 15% on any item or all items, also to make partial award, without any change in the unit price quoted.

7) Quotations *must* be accompanied by descriptive catalogues/leaflets in *triplicate* for the items quoted, which must be in *English*.

8) *To be certified that the goods offered are neither of Israeli origin nor do they contain any Israeli materials in their manufacture.* (Emphasis added)

From:

United Gulf Company
P.O. Box 22218 Safat
Kuwait. (Arabian Gulf)

P.O. Box 205
Cable: Spadmiro   Riyadh, Saudi Arabia

CONTRACT FOR THE DESIGN OF THE EXTENTION
OF THE INSTITUTE OF PUBLIC ADMINISTRATION
BUILDING & LEVELING, FENCING & LANDSCAPING
OF THE SITE IN RIYADH

This contract has been concluded and signed in Riyahd, Saudi Arabia on
——————197 corresponding to ————139 between:

1. The Institute of Public Administration, Riyadh, Saudi Arabia, represented
    by H.E. The General Director of the Institute of Public Administration,
    (hereinafter referred to as the "Institute")
    . . . . .as the FIRST PARTY.

2. The Architects Collaborative Inc., represented by Mr. Louis A. McMillen,
    Mr. William J. Geddis, and Architect Mohamed A. Al-Sabek (hereinafter
    referred to as the consultant)
    . . . . .as the SECOND PARTY.

Introduction:

Whereas the Institute intends to assign the design of the extension of its
buildings, details of which, are given in the attached Appendix together with
leveling, fencing and landscaping of the site shown on the drawings with an
approximate area of 35000 m^2 to a specialized consulting firm, and whereas the
consultant has indicated his willingness to perform this work, and WHEREAS the
Board of management of the Institute by decision number 48/14/13 issued in its
meeting held on 22/1/1394 has approved to assign the work to the Consultant,
hereby agreed as follows:

Article I

The Institute appoints the Consultant to perform the work outlined in
article (2) below and the Consultant accepts to perform such work according to
the conditions and terms set forth in this contract.

. . . .

Article 17

The Consultant shall not in any way perform any functions that will be
contrary to the regulations of the Boycott of Israel Office.

. . . .

Article 26

The contract shall become effective on the date it is signed by the two parties hereto.

FIRST PARTY   *SECOND PARTY*

Fahd Dughaither   Louis A. McMillen   Mohamed A. Al. Sabek
Director General

                                    William J. Geddis
                         For The Architects Collaborative Inc.

_____

   Note: The above agreement was executed by the parties thereto sometime during the year 1975.

APPENDIX D: U.S.
DEPARTMENT OF COMMERCE
EXPORT REPORT FORM

FORM APPROVED: OMB NO. 41-R2305

FORM DIB-621P
(REV. 11-75)

U.S. DEPARTMENT OF COMMERCE
DOMESTIC AND INTERNATIONAL BUSINESS ADMINISTRATION
OFFICE OF EXPORT ADMINISTRATION
WASHINGTON, D.C. 20230

REPORT OF RESTRICTIVE TRADE PRACTICE OR BOYCOTT REQUEST
(For reporting requests defined in § 369.3 of the Export Administration Regulations.)

A. IMPORTANT. It is the policy of the United States to oppose restrictive trade practices or boycotts fostered or imposed by foreign countries against other countries friendly to the United States. All U.S. exporters of articles, materials, supplies, or information, and related export service organizations, (1) are prohibited from taking any action, including the furnishing of information or the signing of agreements, that would have the effect of discriminating against U.S. citizens or firms on the basis of race, color, religion, sex, or national origin; and (2) are encouraged and requested to refuse to take any action, including the furnishing of information or the signing of agreements, that would have the effect of furthering or supporting other types of restrictive trade practices or boycotts against a country friendly to the United States.

Secretary of Commerce

B. Reporting is MANDATORY. *See detailed instructions on back of form.*

C. CONFIDENTIAL. Information furnished herewith is deemed confidential and will not be published or disclosed except as specified in Section 7(c) of the Export Administration Act of 1969 as amended (50 USC app. 2406(c)).

1. Name and Address of U.S. Firm submitting this report:

   Name:

   Address:

   City, State, & Zip:

   Telephone:

2. Are You: *(Check one)*
   ☐ Exporter   ☐ Bank
   ☐ Insurer   ☐ Shipper
   ☐ Forwarder
   ☐ Other _____

   If not exporter, give exporter's:
   Name:
   Address:
   City, State, Zip:

3. To the extent known, give:
   Letter of credit no. _____
   Customer order no. _____
   Exporter's invoice no. _____
   Other identifying marks or numbers _____

4. Name of country(ies) against which request is directed:

5. Name of country initiating request:

6. Date request was received by me/us:

7. The party making the request is:

   Address _____ City & Country _____

8. Specify type of request received and attach copy of document in which it appears:
   a. ☐ Questionnaire   d. ☐ Purchase order   g. ☐ Published import regulation
   b. ☐ Invitation to bid   e. ☐ Contract   h. ☐ Cable or letter
   c. ☐ Trade opportunity   f. ☐ Letter of Credit   i. ☐ Consular request
   j. ☐ Other (Specify) _____

9. If the request relates to a specific transaction, describe the commodities or technical data involved. (The description of the commodity or technical data may conform to the description on the order or to usual commercial terminology, and may, but need not be, in terms of the Commodity Control List or Schedule B.)

Quantity	Description	Value

10. Additional Remarks:

11. Action:
    a. ☐ I/We have **not** complied and will **not** comply with the request for information or action described above.
    b. ☐ I/We have complied with, or will comply with, the request for information or action described above.
    c. ☐ I/We have **not decided** whether I/We shall comply with the request for information or action described above and I/We will inform the Office of Export Administration of my/our decision within 5 business days of making a decision.
    d. ☐ The decision will be made by another party involved in the export transaction. The name of that party is:

12. I certify that all statements and information contained in this report are true and correct to the best of my knowledge and belief.

    Sign here in ink _____   Type or print _____   Date _____
    (Signature of person completing report)   *(Name and title of person whose signature appears on line to left)*

96

Massachusetts Commission
Against Discrimination
McCormack State Office Bldg.
1 Ashburton Place
Boston, Mass. 02108

FOR IMMEDIATE RELEASE   August 15, 1975

The following statement was issued on July 29, 1975, by Glendora M. Putnam, Chairman of the Massachusetts Commission Against Discrimination (MCAD):

"The Commission Against Discrimination has had several requests recently concerning an employer's obligations vis-a-vis employees of the Jewish faith and those policies and restrictions of the Arab nations in doing business with local companies and concerns.

"It has come to the attention of the Commission that, as a result of the Arab policies, certain American firms doing business in the Commonwealth of Massachusetts which employs members of the Jewish faith in managment and other visible positions have taken action with respect to those employees or prospective employees which violates the anti-discrimination laws of the Commonwealth of Massachusetts.

"Any employer who as a direct or indirect result of the Arab boycott discharges or refuses to hire Jews, or discriminates against Jews in compensation or in the terms, conditions or privileges of their employment violates General Laws Chapter 151B. It is an unlawful practice for an employer to exclude a member of the Jewish faith from certain jobs, projects or assignments because of that employee's religious creed or national origin whether such a policy of discrimination is one of the employer's own making or one imposed upon it by a concern with whom the local employer does business.

"The Commission will investigate all complaints arising under these circumstances and, indeed, intends to exercise its authority including its investigatory powers to uncover violations of the foregoing law, and to assure the adherence by Massachusetts employers to non-discriminatory employment policies.

"Any person who feels that his employment has been adversely affected in any way because of his or her religious creed or national origin should contact the Commission Against Discrimination."

PR #41

97

A.C.D. Sales
A.C.S. Industries
Adams Carbide
Air Electric of New York
Ajax Electric
Aled Originals
Albumina
All State Enterprises
Allstate Insurance
Allstate Fire Insurance
Allstate Life Insurance
Alva Museum Replicas
Alva Stone
Alweg Rapid Transit
American Association
American Biltrite Rubber Company
American Box Shook Export
American Committee for Bar Ilan
    University
American Continentle Association
American Dental Manufacturers
American Doll and Toy
American Doll
American Electrical Laboratories
American Electric Power
American Electric Power Services
American Israel Basic Economy
American & Israel Management
American-Israel Cultural Foundation
American-Israel Gas
American-Israel Phosphates

American-Israel Shipping
American Israel World's Flare
American Latex
American Levant Machinery
American-Mediterranean
American Petroleum
American Technion
American Precious Stones
American Roland Food
American Rubber & Chemical
American Shipping
Ames
Ames International
Ampal American
Amerex
Andora
Ander Prost
Anglo Textiles
Ann Marie Sports
A. Plein
A. Asch
Accurate Manufacturers
Admiration
Advance Stores
Aerospace Systems
Ainsbrooke
Airvue
All State Management
Allied Bird
America and Israel Growth Fund
American Bank and Trust Company

This list appeared in full in the New York *Times*, February 27, 1975. For brevity, the terms "Co." and "Inc." have not been printed. The list appearing in the New York *Times* was not in perfect alphabetical order, and the New York *Times'* order is preserved.

American Biltrite
American Bird Food
American Committee for Boystown
    Jerusalem
American Education
    Wesleyan University Press
American Electro-Chemicals
American Israel Public Affairs Com-
    mittee
American Jewish Committee
American Jewish Congress
American Jewish League
American Road Insurance
American Seed and Feed
American Shell Properties
American Society for Relief and
    Immigrants
American Synthetic Rubber
Amirline
Amitone
Ampat
Amtico
Amun Israel
Angle TTTE
Angila
Ann & Edgar Bronfman Foundation
Anti-Defamation League
American Continental
American Association for Jewish Edu-
    cation
Air Products
Atlanta Oxygen
Alger Fund
Amsterdam Overseas
Argus Chemicals
Appliance Buyers Credit
Applied Optics and Mechanics
Aquasol
Ardisco
Aridin
Ashton Valve
Associated Sports
Asthma Nefrin

Asthol
Autolite
Azoentusul
Apparel Industries
Aro Veneers
Artistic Israel Jewelry
Arye Rozenson
Associated Concrete Pipes
Ata
Aveeno

Baltimore Luggage
Banco Americano Israel
Banco
Bayway Terminal Division
Beatties Lighter
Beech Bottom Power
Beechfield Rental Homes
B.C. Morton
Burberrys
Burlington, Inc.
Burgess
B. Weber & Heilbroner
B.C. Morton Foundation
B.C. Morton Financial Corp.
B. Young Baker's Bottle Ready
Baker's Infant Formula
Baltimore Clothes
Basic Systems
Baum Yochin
Bearing Inspection
Beatrice Pocahontas
Belding Chemical
Belding Corticelli
Belding Hausman
Belding Hemingway
Belding Real Estate
Bell Brothers
Bellwood Shoes
Belmont Laboratory
Belvedere
Bennet
Berland

Blue Ridge
M.C. Shoe
B'nai B'rith Lodge
Bomyte
Boston British Prep.
Botany
Bonwit Teller
Brager
Bretz Mining
Brite-Guard
Broadcast Commercial Electronics
Bronco
Brow Beautiful
Brown Vinters
Bruno Scheidt
Building Frames
Bulldog
Business Production Systems
Butternut
A.M. Byers
Begged Or
Belsford Construction
Becker Ryan
Berhman House
Bermanco
Bestform
Bi-Flex
Bischoff Chemicals
Blair House
B&O Cash
Bomher
Bonafide
Botany
Brant
Broadstreet
Boyar Kessler
Brager
Brooklyn Apartments
B.R. Baker
Bryan Oldsmobile
Bulova Foundation
Bulova

California AM
Calbro
Calonlympic Glove
Captina
Carmel Wine
Cardeff
Carrollwood Construction
Ce De Candy
Central Appalachian
Central Coal
Central Electric
Central Ohio Coal
Central Arms
Central Operating
Central Paper
Central Queens Savings
C.G. Electronics
Evans
Charles Center Parking
Charlesmont Park
Chemstrand Overseas
Citadel Life
Clayton Hall
Colonial Crest
Colt
Compain Occidental
Compass
Concrete Pipe
Consolidated Molded Products
Consolidated Laundries
Consolidated Frees
Construction Aggregates
Continental Imports
Continental Made
Continental Ore
Consumers Pain
Corroplast
Cos. Manufacturers
Country Tweeds
Cross Country Life
Chossland Realty
Caliente

Callanan Slag
Calvert
Capital for Israel
Capitol Products
Capri
Carewell Trading
Carey Cadillac
Carlisle Shoe
Charm Step Shoe
Cheshire
Chelsea Publications
Chemstone
Chevinal
Chicago Specialty Manufacturing
Chicago Transport Service
Chime
Classics International
Clerespan
Coastal Footwear Corporation
Coca-Cola
Coldspot
Colorsilk
Columbia Aquarium
Comet
Concordant
Connecticut General Life
Connecticut Mutual Life
Constance Spry
Consul
Converse
Corsair
Corticelli
Cortina
Corwell
Council of Federation and Welfare
    Funds
Cover Girl Shoe
Crosby Valve
Curtis Industries
Computer Direction Fund
Council of Jewish Federation and
    Welfare

Calfos
Cong. for Jewish Culture
Catalytic Construction
Club Mediterrane
Columbia Broadcasting
Cat's Paw
Curtis Noll
Cuyahoga
Cuyahoga Lime
Cyclone

Dayco
DBI
Dearborn
Dopt
Dominion Shoe
Donner-Hanna
Donovan
Douglas Shoe
Daiper
Dan Hotel
Dwyer Baker
Dynatech
Duncan Foods
Dadeland
Dalila
Dane
Daroff
Davinci Records
Oscar Davis
Dav's Lab
Deedfield
Derby Sportswear
DeSoto
Development Corporation of Israel
Diamond Distributors
Douglas Fund
Direct Jewelry
Diversified Builders
Dome Chemical
Druid Valley Apartments

D.S. Gordon
Dumont Emerson

Eagle Shipping
Eagle Signal
East Point
E.C. Publishing
The Ecuadorian Fruit Imp.
Edmondson Village
E.W. Bliss
Extron Trading
Eterna "27"
Evan Picone
Eveleith Taconite
Export Procurement
Eagle
E.C. Baum
E.J. Korvette
Eagle Shipping
Eastern Shoe
Ecco
Econoline
Electric Equipment
Electro Flashcote
Electronic Components & Devices
Eisenberg
Electro Chemical Engineering
Electro Optical
Electro Spark
Elegencia
Elemek of Israel
Elliot Import
Elliot Knitwear
Ellis Realty
Emanuel Blumenfrucht
Emerson
Electrunite
Elliot Publ.
Eltra
Emu
Enamelite
Encyclopedia Judaica Research
Endura

English American Tailor
Entubul
Engelhard
Elox
Euclid Orion
Elco
Emkol
Empire Brushes
Empire Pencil
Empire Rainwear
Empire Stamp
Empire Twine
Ernst Bischoff

Fairbanks Whitney
Fama-Corp.
Famous Raincoat
Fairbanks Morse
Fairlane
Falcons
Famous Authors
Fanta
Farrow
Farm Pipe
Feuchtwanger
Fidelity Service
Filtered Resin
Flaming Foam
Fleet Maintenance
Ford Bacon & Davis
Forum Realty
Foster Grant
Foothill
Franklin
Frederick M. Gottlieb
Freeman Helpern
Fullcut
Federation of Jewish Philanthropies
Femicin
Ferrobord
Fiamma
Fidelity Mutual
Fingertip Tans

Flagg

Flagg-Utica

Fleetwood

Fluride-Vitamin

Fomoco

Ford

Ford "D"

Foreign Trade Exchange

Forest City Materials

Formit Rogers

Fortune Shoe

Farband

Financial Institutions Growth

Ford Life

Four Roses

Frank Brothers

Penn Feinstein

Frankfort

Fresca

Fromm & Sichel

Fund American

Galvite General Chem.

General Thread

General Tire and Rubber*

General Wine

Genesco

George D. Ropper

Galis Manuf.

Guide-Line

Galaxy Homes

Gamewell

General Shoe

George M. Black

George Carpenter

George Ehert

Gilpin Construction

Glazier

Glenco

Glickman

Glenoit Mills

Global Tours

Great Universal Stores

Golden Bear

Gesco

Gidding Jenny

Gilberton

Glacier

Granite State Rubber

Graphic Systems

Gorelle

Gotham Knitting

Granco

Green Leaf Textiles

Gresca

Gristede

Grunner

Gulton

Gypsum Carrier

H.C. Bohack

H. Green

H&M Wilson

Hadassah

Harodite

Harley

Harris & Frank

Harrop Ceramic

Huntington Creek

Hudson Pulp

House of Worsted Tex.

H.V. Spectorman

Harry Winston

Harville

Hassenfeld

Hengeman-Harris

---

*General Tire and Rubber, in March 1976, admitted that it had paid $150,000 to a firm in Lebanon to remove the company's name from the blacklist. Jerusalem *Post*, March 28, 1976.

Helena Rubinstein
Helene Curtis
Henninger
Henry J
Henry Hose
Herbert Marnoro
Herman Hollander
H.M. Grauer
Holy Land Marble
Homart
Homan
Home Insurance
Hornell Beers
H.S. Caplin
Hartz
Hawaii-Kai
Heelin Toe
Henri Bendel
Hertz Hickory
Hill Samuel
Hillwood Shoe
Holt Beranek Newman
Home Instruments
House of Seagram
Huggins Young
Humboldt
Hunter-Wilson
Holley
Houdry

I. Miller
I. Milton
Israel Fund Distributors
Inch-Marked
Independence Acceptance
Industrial Computers
Information Systems
Ingenieria Y. Construciones Kaiser
Inland Credit
Innes
Instant Patent Leather
Int. Dental Products
Inter-Line

Interstate Shoe
Imperial Export
Imported Brands
Import from Israel
Imported Glass
Indiana Franklin
Indiana and Michigan Electric
Industrial Finance
Inland Wallpaper
Instrument System
Intercontinental Importers
Intercontinental Transportation
International Latex
International Paper
International Pipe
Interocean Advertising
Interocean Radio
Isaac J. Shalom
Isadore Ash
Israel American Bank
Israel-American Oil
Israel American Shipping
Israel Artcraft
Israel Coin
Israel Creations
Israel Commodities
International Packers
Israel Designs
Israel Economic
Israel Gloves
Israel Import
Israel Investors
Israel Numismatic
Israel Purchasing
Israel Philatellic
Israel Razor
Israel Religious Art
Israel Wine
Intimate Crystaline Spray Mist
Intimco
Investors Overseas
Israel Alabama Wire
Israel American Diversified

Israel Education Fund
Israel Funds Management
Israel Miami
Israel Securities

Jablo Plastics
J.A. Johnston
J. Genach
J.M. Cook
J.M. Wood
Joseph Meyerhoff
Joseph Savion
Julius Klein
Juniorit
Jaques Foreigner
Jacquith
Jefferson Travis
Jerry Silverman
Jerry Marks
Jessop Steel
J. Gerber
Joseph E. Seagram
J. Levine Religious Supplies
Jordan Manufacturers
Josam Tailors
Joseph Brancroft
Jewish War Veterans
J.K. Cook
Janbra
Jewish Welfare Fund
Jarman
Jeryl Lighting
John Hardy
Johnston and Murphy
Joint Distribution Committee
Jolie Madame
Judea Art
Julius Kesler Distillery

K. Kettleman
K&S Metal
Kluger
Klutznick Kook

Korday
Kordeen
Kraus
Kaiser
Kaiser Frazer
Kanauha Valley Power
Kaufman
Keniworth Park
Kensington Realty
Kenneby Cabot
Kennebec
Kennedy Galleries
Kentucky Power
Keystone Controls
Kingsport Utilities
Kelita Sportswear
Kenmore
Kings Country Trust
Kendall
Kingsbord
Kleven Shoe
Knomark
Knopf

Lawrence Schacht
Learning Materials
Leather Palm
Leff Foundation
Lemberg Foundation
Leumi
L.Grief
La Dolce
Lady Esquire
Lazard
Larsan
Leeds Music
Lee Filter
Leidesdorf Foundation
Lemayne
Leon Israel
Leonard Construction
Lewis Prod.
L. Feibelman

Labor Zionist Organization
Litwin
Lexim
Liberia Mining
Liberty Industrial Park
Lilly Mills
Lincoln Mercury Dealer Leasing
Lipschutz & Gutwirth
Locore
Loft
Love Pat
Lewitt Yarn
Leyland (U.S.A.)
L.H. Lincoln
Lifetime Foam Products
Lochwood Apartments
Lock Joint
Loewengart
London Star Diamond
Lorca
Lord & Bishop
Lord & Taylor
L. Sonneborn
Luna Duval
Lyon Import

Madeira Knits
Majestic Specialties
Macco
Machinery Trading
Mororola
Motorola Inc.
Motor Ways
Multicut
Murray Hill Lodge
Murphy
Mutual Life
Musher Foundation
Mackintosh
Memphili Maritime Overseas
Marquette Tool
Martin International
Martin Wolman

Marmara
Mass. Mutual Life Insurance
Mattique
Mate
Mayfair
Mediterranean Agency
Meritt-Chapman-Scott
Merk Ross
Matalock
Metropolis Brewery
Metropolitan Savings
M. Firestone
M. Hausman
Miles California
Miles Laboratories
Mittenberg & Samton
Milton J. Fisher
Minkus Midwest
Minkus Pub.
Minkus Stamp
M. Lowenstein
M.L. Rothschild
Motor Dee Textile
Monarch Fire Insurance
Monarch Wine
Monsanto
Moore and Thompson
Morgenstern
Major Blouse
Mallernees
Mannequin Shoe
Mansco
Maryland Club
Mazon
Mcgregor Doniger
Mechanical Mirror
Metal Lumber
Meteor
Metropolitan Council
Meyer Brothers
Mirco
Minute Maid
Minerals and Chemicals

Missouri Rogers
Modern Orthopedic
Monsieur Balmain
Moondrops Moisturinzing Bath Oil
Moondrops Moisture Lipstick
Manhattan Shirt
Miami Oxygen

Nitro
North Point Land
Nannette
Nassau Brassiere
National Steel
National Brewery
National Dynamics
National Emblem
National Plastic
National Shoe
New England Mutual
Newark Ohio Co.
New West Optic
New York Merchandise
Niles and Bement
Nashville Ave. Realty
Nationwide Shoe
NBC
National Committee Religious
    Advisory Council
National Council of Jewish Women
National Jewish Welfare Board
National Spinning
National Worsted Miles
National Yarn
Natural Wonder Medicated Total Skin
    Lotion
Nilatil
Noonan
Norry Electric
National Council for Jewish Education
National Union Electric
Noxon

Ocean Clippers
Ocean Transport

Ofer Style
Ohawa
Ohio Power
Olympic Glove
Omni Fabrics
Onan
Orco
Oriental Export
Orisco
Orlite Engineering
Overseas Discount
Otto Preminger Film
Ogma Productions
Overseas African Construction
Overseas Public Utilities
Owens Illinois
Old Colony Tar
Oak Engineering

Pacific Diamond
Pacific Installers
Pacific Dredging
Pacific Gypsum
Pagoda Arts
Palestine Economic
Pama Properties
Panto Mines
Pavelle Trading
PEC Diamond
Peltours
Permanente
Perrine Realty
Pennsburg
Pennmutual Life
Philipp Bros.
Philadelphia International
Philadelphia National Bank
Phil Silvers Co.
Phoenix Assurance
Phoenix Mutual Life
Phonovision
Pilot Radio
Pioneer Women's Labor Zionist Organ.
Plastimold

Plax
Portland Copper
Pacific Mills
Pacifics Polymers
Palestine Endowment Funds
Pantheon
Patina
Paul Jones Co.
Paul Masson
Pearl Import
Penn. Coal, Coke
Permanent Steamship
Permanent Trucking
Perveline
Pervinal
4 Pet Shop
Pharma-Craft
Philco
Philipps Bros.
Phoenix
Policlean Whirlpool
Pohocel
Pratt & Whitney
Phenix Aluminum
Philipp Bros. India
Progress Webster
Perfect
Princess Marcella Borghese
Professional Library Service
Prospect
Provident Mutual
Pub
Puerto Rican Cars
Pyramid Shoe
Poter & Johnston
Premiers
Princeton Knitting

Quick Ease
Quincy Compressor
Quiet Heet

R.A.M. Apparel
Realton Electronics
Ralli
Rassco
Rauland
Rotosin
Roseach
Rothley
Rudin
Russco
Republic
Republic Productions
Revlon
Reynolds Construction
R.H. Cole
Richelieu
Rio da la Plata Trading
Ripel Shoe
Robert R. Nathan Assoc.
Robison-Anton
Rockwood Sprinkler
RCA
Ranchero
Random House
Rasso-Israel
Ravne Delman
Ready
Real Gold
Realistic
Replique
Republic Shoe
Republic Steel
Republic Supply
Reserve Mining
Religious Zionists of America
Rumac
Ridgefield
Rigid-Floor
Rigid-Rib
River Terminal Rail
Laurence Rockefeller Assoc.

Roger Kent
Royal Lynne

S.H. Kress
Schacht Foundation
Schacht Steel
Seaboard
Seal King
San Diamond Knitting
Samuel Adire
San Rafael Cayes
Scherr Tumica
S.D. Leidesdorf
Sealanes International
Seven Star
Sears Roebuck
Simpson Sears
Seneca Mail
Seminari South
Sharon Palestime
Shawninigan
Shulsinger
Shunt Lamp
Sifrei-Israel
Sinclair & Valentine Inc.
Skye
S.M. Elowsky
Solcoor
Sol
Southern Textiles
South Bend
Southern Permanente
Southern Shipping
Southland Mail
Spanel-Foundation
Sporteens
Sport togs
Spraying Systems
Stanalchem
Standard Magnesium
Standard Triumph

Stanley Warner
Stapling Machines
State Mutual Life
Stearns Roger
Senty Shoe
721 Corp.
Shapiro Foundation
Sigma
Silver Slick
1616 Building
Snow
Sommer and Kaufman
Soverign Shoe
Spartan
Sprite
Staples and Specialties Int.
Sholem Aleichem Folk Institute
Southern Steamship Agency
Sterling Die
Stone Charitable Foundation
Stone Container
Stowal Silk Spool
Susan Mercantile
Sweeping Beauty
Stone and Forsyth
Straus Duparguet
Sumner Chemical
Sunwear
Surlon & Israel Foreign Trade
Surveys and Research
Swiss-Israel Bank

T. Noonan & Sons
Tiroa Operational Satellites
Tab
Tankore
Takamine Laboratories
Taller & Cooper
Taro Pharmacies
Tartan
Tatra Sheep Cheese

Tel Aviv Import.
Terminal Freight Handling
Three Lions Publishers
Tinagara Novelties
Titan
Toledo Machine
Topps Chewing Gum Company
Torczyner
Town-Moor
Town & Country Developers
T. Parker Host
Trans. Music
Treisser Tours
Tri-County Shopping Center
Taunus
Tawny
Tectrol Service
Temco International
Thames Vans
"That Man" Spray
Thayer Laboratories
Thomas J. Webb
Tintex
Tip Top
Tar Distilling
Top Brass
Touch & Glow
Triangle Shoes
Trustee Funds
Trust-T-Post
Tuk-Town Distributors
Turover Mill
Twin Branch Rail
Tzell Tours

Union Bag-Camp Paper
United Associates
US Near East Lab
US Glass
United Supply
University Microfilm
Universal Rundle
US Wallboard Machinery

Utility Appliance
U.S. Vitamin
"Ultima II" Makeup
Ultramat
Union Drawn Steel
United Investors
United HIAS
Union of American Hebrew Congrega-
        tions
Ultra Chemical
US Peroxygen

V.J. Elmore
Valcar Rentals
Valentine Shoe
Valley Gold
Valmore Leather
Vanees
Vapo Nefrin
Vee's Bird Feeds
Vega Trading
Vence Iron
Vent Vert
Victor Fischel
Victrola
Virginia Dyeing
Vision-Vent
Vaco
Vacumizer
Victoria Vogue
Vinango
Vintage Wines

Warwick Electric
Warwick
Welbilt
Walker Land
Weldon Mills
Waldman Assoc.
West Coast Line
Western Woods
West Virginia Fower
Westview Apartments

West View Shopping Center
Wheeling Electric
W.H. Dougherty Refinery
Whistleclean
Wilhelm Band
Williams Diamond
William H. Wanamaker
Willys Overland
Wincharger
Windsor Fower
W.C. Thainwall
Wetherogue
Wedge Lock
Whirlpool
Whitehall
Whitehouse & Hardy
Witco
William Olroyd
Workmen's Circle
Whitfield Chemicals
Winkler Credit

Woodbridge Construction
Woodcraft

X-Thru-Coat
Xerox
X-Trube

Yeshiva University Community
York Fund
Young-Timer Shoe
Yorktown Industries
Yaski

Zenith
Zim Israel Lines
Zoller Casting
Zenith Shoe
Zephyr
Zodiac
Zunio-Altman
Zionist Organization of America

California: Bank of America, and Wells Fargo Bank (San Francisco)

New York: First National City Bank, Chase Manhattan Bank, Chemical Bank, Bankers Trust, and Morgan Guaranty Trust

Illinois: First National Bank of Chicago and Continental Bank

Minnesota: First National Bank of Minneapolis and First National Bank of St. Paul

Ohio: Akron National Bank, Central National Bank and National City Bank (Cleveland), First National Bank of Dayton

Pennsylvania: Philadelphia National Bank

Texas: Texas Commerce Bank and Bank of the Southwest (Houston)

Wisconsin: Marine National Exchange Bank (Milwaukee)

Allegations in a press release made by the Anti-Defamation League on March 11, 1976.

Books and Articles

Anatawbi, Munzer Fayek. *Arab Unity in Terms of Law.* The Hague: Martinus Nijhoff, 1963.

Bahti, James H. *The Arab Economic Boycott of Israel.* Washington, D.C.: The Brookings Institution, 1967.

Banerji, J. K. *The Middle East in World Politics.* Calcutta: The World Press Private, 1960.

Bernstein, Marver. *The Politics of Israel.* Princeton, N.J.: Princeton University Press, 1957.

Bollack, Leon. *La Question des Sanctions Economiques en Cas de Violation du Droit International.* (17th National Peace Congress) Paris: Clermont-Ferrand, 1911.

––––. *Comment Tuer La Guerre: La Loi Mondiale de Boycottage Douanier.* Paris: Chez L'Auteur, 1912.

Bouve, C. L. "National Boycott as an International Delinquency," *AJIL* 28, no. 19 (January 1934).

Brown, E. A. "Boycott in International Law," *Canadian Bar Review*, 11, no. 325 (May 1934).

Business International. "Coping with the Arab Boycott of Israel." Management Monographs. New York: Business Internation, 1964.

Clark, Evans, ed. *Boycotts and Peace: A Report by the Committee on Economic Sanctions.* New York: Harper and Brothers, 1932.

Coleman, Clarence L., Jr. "Boycott Not Religious, Arabs Tell State Department." *Issues*, (Spring 1962): 79-80.

Comment. "The Arab-Israeli War and International Law." *Harvard International Law Journal* 9, no. 232 (Spring 1968).

Cremeans, Charles D. *The Arabs and the World.* New York: Frederick A. Praeger, 1963.

Dagan, A. "The Arab Boycott." In *Israel Yearbook 1966* (Jerusalem: Israel Yearbook Publications, 1966).

De Crispigny, A. R. C., and R. T. McKinnell. "The Nature and Significance of Economic Boycott." *The South African Journal of Economics,* December 1960.

Dworkin, Susan. "The Japanese and the Arab Boycott." *Near East Report,* suppl. (October 1968): 11-13.

Eban, Abba. "The Answer to Arab Boycott." In *The Israel Yearbook 1966* (Jerusalem: Israel Yearbook Publications, 1966), pp. 19-21.

————. *Voice of Israel.* New York: Horizon Press, 1957.

Egyptian Society of International Law. *Egypt and the United Nations.* New York: Manhattan Publishing Co., 1957.

Ellis, Harry B. "The Arab-Israeli Conflict Today." In American Assembly, *The United States and the Middle East.* Englewood Cliffs, N.J.: Prentice-Hall, 1964.

Forster, Arnold. "The Arab Boycott: An Interim Report." *ADL Bulletin,* June 1975.

Friedmann, W. "Some Impacts of Social Organization on International Law." *AJIL* 50, no. 475 (1956).

Gervasi, Frank. *The Case for Israel.* New York: The Viking Press, 1967.

Gold, Bertram H. "Americans Against Americans: Playing the Arab Game." *Hadassah Magazine* (June 1975): 9, 29-30.

Gross, Leo. "Passage Through the Suez Canal of Israel-Bound Cargo and Israel Ships." *AJIL* 51, no. 530 (1957).

Harkabi, Y. *Emdat Ha-aravim Besihsuh Yisroel-Arav.* The Arabs' Position in their Conflict with Israel. Tel Aviv: Dvir Co., 1968.

Holcombe, C. "Chinese Exclusion and the Boycott." *Outlook* (December 30, 1905): 1071-72.

Hunsberger, W. S. *Japan and the United States in World Trade.* New York: Harper and Row, 1964.

Hurewitz, J. C. *Middle East Politics.* London: Pall Mall Press, 1969.

Hyde, C. C. "Boycott as a Sanction of International Law." *Political Science Quarterly* 48, no. 211 (June 1933).

————. *International Law.* Vol. 3. Boston: Little, Brown and Co., 1947.

———— and L. B. Wehle. "The Boycott in Foreign Affairs." *AJIL* 27, no. 1 (1933).

Iskandar, Marwan. "Arab Boycott of Israel." *Middle East Forum* 36 (October 1960): 27-30.

Kerr, Malcolm. *The Arab Cold War: A Study of Ideology in Politics, 1958-1967.* London: Oxford University Press, 1967.

Khalil, M. *The Arab States and the Arab League.* Vol. 2. Beirut: Khayats, 1955.

Khouri, Fred J. *The Arab-Israeli Dilemma.* Syracuse, N.Y.: Syracuse University Press, 1968.

Laferriere, J. *Le Boycott et Le Droit International.* Paris: A Pedone, 1910.

Lauterpacht, H. "Boycott in International Relations." *British Yearbook of International Law* 14, no. 125 (1933).

——. *The Function of Law in the International Community.* Hamden, Conn.: Archon Books, 1966.

"List of Boycott Recommendations." *Economic Review of the Arab World,* no. 2 (February 1967).

MacDonald, Robert W. *The League of Arab States: A Study in the Dynamics of Regional Organization.* Princeton, N.J.: Princeton University Press, 1965.

McDougal, Myres S., and W. Michael Reisman. "Rhodesia and the United Nations: The Lawfulness of International Concern." *AJIL* 62, no. 1 (1968).

Mogannam, M. E. T. *The Arab Woman.* London: Hubert Joseph, 1937.

Moore, John Bassett. "The New Isolation." *AJIL* 27, no. 607 (1933).

Mourad, Rashad. "The Arab Boycott—Its Application." *American-Arab Trade Newsletter,* (Spring-Summer, 1966): 5-6.

Oppenheim, L. *International Law.* Vol. 2 (7th ed., edited by H. Lauterpacht). London: Longmans, Green and Co., 1952.

Orchard, Dorothy J. "China's Use of the Boycott as a Political Weapon." *The Annals of the American Academy of Political Science* (November 1930): 253.

Palmer, R. R., and J. Colton, *A History of the Modern World.* New York: Alfred A. Knopf, 1965.

Peretz, Don. *The Middle East Today.* New York: Holt, Rinehart and Winston, 1963.

Remba, Oded. "The Arab Boycott: A Study in Total Economic Warfare." *Midstream* 6, no. 3 (Summer 1960): 40-55.

Remer, C. F. *A Study of Chinese Boycotts.* Baltimore: Johns Hopkins Press, 1933.

Roudot, Pierre. "Arab Boycott as Myth." *New Outlook* 6, no. 5 (June 1963): 17-24.

Safran, Nadav. *The United States and Israel.* Cambridge: Harvard University Press, 1963.

Schwarzenberger, G. *A Manual of International Law.* 5th ed. London: Stevens and Sons, 1967.

Seabury, Paul. "The League of Arab States: Debacle of a Regional Arrangement." *International Organization* (February 1949): 633-42.

Seferiades, St. P. *Reflexions Sur Le Boycottage en Droit International.* Paris: Arthur Rousseau, 1912.

Shefer, M. "The Effect of the Arab-Israeli Rupture on the Economy of the Arab Countries." *New Outlook* 7, no. 9 (November-December 1964): 4-16.

Sohn, Louis B., ed. *Basic Documents of the United Nations.* 2d ed. Brooklyn: The Foundation Press, 1968.

———. *Cases on United Nations Law.* Brooklyn: The Foundation Press, 1967.

Takayanagi, Kenzo. "On the Legality of the Chinese Boycott." *Pacific Affairs* 5, no. 10 (October 1932): 855-62.

Teilhac, Ernest. *Economie Politique Pour Les Arabes.* Paris: R. Pichon and R. Durand-Auzias, 1960.

"The Boycott of Israel Office," *Arab Economist* (April 1975): 36 ff.

Toynbee, Arnold J. *Survey of International Affairs, 1934.* London: Oxford University Press, 1934.

Vickers, Ray. "Israel's Second Front." *Wall Street Journal,* December 30, 1974.

Weigand, Robert E. "The Arab League Boycott of Israel." *Michigan State University Business Topics* (Spring 1968): 74-80.

Woolbert, R. G. "Pan Arabism and the Palestine Problem." *Foreign Affairs* (January 1938): 317.

Periodicals and Government Regulations and Circulars

Britain and Israel, no. 41 (February 1975).

Business International, May 31, 1957.

Business Week, March 17, 1975.

Circular Letter (Federal Reserve Board). December 12, 1975.

Circular No. 21 (U.S. Commerce Secretary), November 26, 1975.

Daily News Bulletin (Jewish Telegraph Agency), various issues.

For the Record (Arab Information Agency, New York), April 25, 1966.

Foreign Commerce Weekly (U.S. Department of Commerce), March 5, 1956.

"General Principles for Boycott of Israel," June 1972, League of Arab Countries, General Secretariat, Head Office for Boycott of Israel, Damascus.

Middle East Record 1961. Jerusalem: Reuven Shiloah Research Institute, 1961.

Midstream, April 1975.

Near East Report 9, no. 26 (December 28, 1965); supplement, May 1965; special survey, August 1967.

New Outlook (Middle East monthly) 4, no. 5 (March-April 1961): 33-38.

Reports by Government Agencies and Minority Groups

American Jewish Congress, *American Law vs. The Arab Boycott.* Memorandum to the president of the United States, April 1975.

American Jewish Congress, *The Arab Campaign Against American Jews* (1956).

Anti-Defamation League, B'nai B'rith. *Japan's Foreign Trade and the Arab Boycott of Israel.* New York: Anti-Defamation League, January 1968.

Egyptian Official Journal, no. 36 (April 8, 1950).

General Union of the Arab Chambers of Commerce, Industry and Agriculture. *Arab Boycott of Israel: Its Grounds and Its Regulations.* Beirut, 1959.

Government of Japan. *Japanese Economic Statistics.* Tokyo: Economic Planning Agency, 1966.

"Japan Air Lines—Recent Developments." Memorandum from Phil Baum, Director of the Commission of International Affairs (CIA), American Jewish Congress, to the Congress' chapter and division presidents, chapter and division CIA Chairmen, regional directors, Regional Councils and Staff, February 28, 1973.

Palestine Royal Commission Report. Commission Mandate Documents 5479, London, 1937.

Presidents of Major American Jewish Organizations. *A Report on the Arab Boycott Against Americans.* New York, 1958.

Public Affairs Institute. "Regional Development for Regional Peace." Mimeographed. Washington, D.C., 1957.

World Jewish Congress, *Evidence of the Arab War in Peacetime Against Israel.* Tel Aviv: Hadfus Haklali, 1957.

U.S., League of Nations, and UN Documents

Assistant Secretary of State Thurston B. Morton to Senator Herbert Lehman of New York, December 15, 1953.

Department of State Bulletin, September 9, 1939, p. 208; *Department of State Bulletin* 36, no. 596 (1957).

General Assembly. Resolution 500 (V). GAOR, V, Supp. 20A (A/1775/Add.1), May 18, 1951, New York, p. 2.

General Assembly. Resolution 2131 (XX). GAOR, V, Supp. 14 (A/6014), December 21, 1965, New York, pp. 11-12.

League of Nations. *Report of the Commission of Inquiry.* Doc. C, 663, M. 320, 1932 (VII).

Security Council. Resolution 2322.(S/2322), September 1, 1951, New York.

UN Document S/PV.664. Verbatim record of the six-hundred sixty-fourth meeting of the Security Council, March 20, 1954, New York.

United Nations. *Treaty Series* 15 (1948), New York.

U.S. Congress, Senate, *Congressional Record*, 86th Congress, 2nd Sess., 1960, p. 8976.

United States Treaties and Other International Acts Series, no. 2290. Washington, D.C.: Government Printing Office, 1951.

DAN S. CHILL is a corporate attorney working in Israel. Prior to his Aliyah to Israel in September, 1975, he served as a litigation attorney in the Boston law firm of Brown, Rudnick, Freed and Gesmer.

In addition to publishing a Case Note on Air Law/Conflict of Laws in *Harvard International Law Journal* 9, no. 286 (1968), Mr. Chill is the author of the Commonwealth of Massachusetts' amicus curiae legal memorandum served upon Roman Rudenko, procurator general of the Soviet Union, on behalf of Mikhail Leviev, an imprisoned Soviet Jew.

Mr. Chill, who commenced his research on the Arab Boycott of Israel in 1964, has lectured extensively in the northeastern United States on the Boycott, has served as a consultant on the Arab Boycott to various nonprofit organizations, and has assisted in the drafting of federal and state legislation in the United States directly related to the Boycott.

Mr. Chill received his B.A. degree, magna cum laude, from New York University and was elected to Phi Beta Kappa. He received his M.P.A. from Harvard University's John F. Kennedy School of Government and his J.D. from the Harvard Law School.

ARAB OIL: Impact on Arab Nations and Global Implications
edited by Naiem A. Sherbiny
and Mark A. Tessler

THE GATT LEGAL SYSTEM AND WORLD TRADE DIPLOMACY
Robert E. Hudec

ISRAEL AND IRAN: Bilateral Relationships and Effect on
the Indian Ocean Basin
Robert B. Reppa, Sr.

ISRAEL'S DEVELOPMENT COOPERATION WITH AFRICA,
ASIA, AND LATIN AMERICA
Shimeon Amir, foreword by
Abba Eban

POLITICAL PARTIES IN ISRAEL: The Evolution of Israeli Democracy
David M. Zohar

SAUDI ARABIA AND OIL DIPLOMACY
Sheikh Rustum Ali

SOVIET POLICY TOWARD THE MIDDLE EAST SINCE 1970[*]
Robert O. Freedman

[*]Also available as a Praeger Special Studies Student Edition